DISCIPLE OF THE GODS

DISCIPLE
OF THE GODS

A biography of
Erich von Däniken

by Peter Krassa

Translated by David Koblick

W. H. ALLEN · LONDON
A Howard & Wyndham Company
1978

IN MEMORIAM
my valiant mother

CONTENTS

INTRODUCTION

Erich von Däniken—the unknown being. Who really knows him? How can he be truly evaluated? As a modern Schliemann?* A devious charlatan? Is he an idealist? Or a frenzied fanatic?

Opinions about EvD—his initials indicate the man—are varied. Some even see him as a straightforward truth-seeker, deeply religious as only a heretic can be.

But do all these descriptions apply to one and the same person? Surely there must be a man, a human being, to be found under this kaleidoscopic exterior.

Erich von Däniken is no stereotype, not a cliché-figure. Unfortunately, he has been made into one. The mass media are largely to blame for this fact. They operate in an environment of snapshots, and show Däniken by the flashes of a strobe-lamp. So, what you read, see and hear about him are only reflections of the person: sometimes positive, mostly negative.

His image has been constantly distorted. Often it is drawn badly on purpose; prejudice is confused with objectivity. Casual glimpses in the form of interviews or brief conversations thus remain the only portrayal of the person Erich von Däniken available to the uninformed public. Obviously, and sad to say, the portrait is a retouched one.

Is it surprising then that opinions about the most controversial of post-war authors are so divergent? So, what is he, really? A revolutionary of ideas with a fertile imagination? A petty plagiarist? An unprincipled outlaw? Or simply: a fraud?

There is really no simple answer.

The picture of Erich von Däniken, 42-year-old Swiss from the town

* Heinrich Schliemann, 1822–1890. German lay archaeologist who discovered the buried ruins of Troy.

of Zofingen, is impossible to fit into a frame. His character is multi-faceted, complicated, and yet as open and transparent as the man we *think* we know. EvD an unknown being? Not at all. That is why this book was written. When you have read it, you will know him—you will feel that he is your best friend!

This book is not just one person's subjective estimate of Däniken. It is not enthusiastic praise for a 'Superman', or condemnation of a scoundrel. Däniken is neither one nor the other, and is certainly not the popular stereotype he is represented to be.

People whom I know—acquaintances as well as close friends—have their say in these pages. They provide an 'X-ray view' of the successful author, reproducing impressions and experiences stemming from contacts with Däniken. Subjectively of course, in each individual deposition, but absolute in their entirety.

This portrait, composed of many aspects and opinions of Erich von Däniken, shows the man beneath the image, the person, until now, hidden from the public.

At this point I would like to express thanks to all those who contributed their advice and suggestions toward the compilation of this book. My especial thanks to those in the front rank, the key figures in these pages. I introduce them here briefly, and so that none should feel either favoured or demoted, in alphabetical order.

Twelve persons who really know Erich von Däniken.

JOSEF F. BLUMRICH: Austrian, 64. Fifteen years in charge of NASA's Systems Layout Division. Worked with Wernher von Braun on both the Saturn and Apollo projects. Holder of numerous patents in rocket construction and related fields. Blumrich is an aero-mechanical engineer, married, with three sons. During his NASA period, lived and worked in Huntsville, Alabama. Pensioned in June 1974, and lives today in Laguna Beach, California.

Däniken first came to Blumrich's attention when he received as a gift EvD's first book, *Chariots of the Gods?*, and at first dismissed the concepts contained therein as utter nonsense. But the Biblical passage analysing the report of the prophet Ezekiel fascinated him. Suddenly Däniken's suppositions appeared to Blumrich in a new light. From several versions of the Biblical text the NASA engineer reconstructed the ostensible 'Glory of God', and came up with an extra-terrestrial landing module. He wrote a book about it, *The Spaceships of Ezekiel*, which corroborated—at least in part—Däniken's hypotheses.

THEO BOS: Dutch, 35. Worked on ocean liners for several years, later as an hotelier. Presently employed in the foreign exchange division of a Swiss bank. Divorced, one son. Bos first became acquainted with Däniken 17 years ago, when they were co-workers aboard a Dutch ship. He is numbered among Däniken's oldest friends.

EDUARDO B. CHAVES: Portuguese, 25. He has a variety of interests, lives and studies in Rio de Janeiro, working there as a journalist and lay archaeologist. Single. Met Däniken five years ago in Rio, when EvD was on one of his expeditions. Chaves gave him an assortment of evidential photographs, which were included in EvD's book *My World in Pictures* (*Meine Welt in Bildern* in the German edition). Däniken reciprocated by inviting Chaves to Switzerland in 1974.

ELISABETH VON DÄNIKEN: German, 40 years young. Met her husband when both were employed in hotel occupations. Later, she and EvD leased the Hotel Rosenhügel in Davos. Today she is 'only' a housewife in the Zürich surburb Bonstetten. Married to Däniken for seventeen years, she presented him with two children: Peterli (the two-month-old infant died tragically in a nursing home) and Cornelia, now fourteen.

OTTO VON DÄNIKEN: Swiss, 44. EvD's older brother. Lives in Bern, where he owns and manages a flourishing TV and radio repair service. Married, one daughter.

WILLI DÜNNENBERGER: Swiss, 23. Became EvD's secretary and archivist after completing an education in business administration. Travels widely with Däniken, is unmarried and he hopes, childless. Described by those who know him well—by me, for instance—as a 'living computer'. Treasured by his employer for this quality and for his reliability. Dünnenberger's precision can be explained by the fact that he was born in Schaffhausen, the city of watchmakers. Lives now where he works, in Bonstetten.

WALTER ERNSTING: German, 57. Free-lance writer. Preferred theme, Science Fiction. Is co-author of the future-adventure series 'Perry Rhodan', translated and read all over the world. Many of Ernsting's novels—written mainly under the pen-name *Clark Darlton* —dealt with some of Däniken's hypotheses as early as the fifties. Met EvD in 1968, travelled together to America in 1974. Married, a son and a daughter. Lives in Ainring, Bavaria.

GERHARD GADOW: German, 26. Author of the widely-discussed paperback *Erinnerungen an die Wirklichkeit*,* in which Gadow accuses

* *Memories of Actuality*, a sarcastic word-play on the German title of EvD's first book *Erinnerungen an die Zukunft* (*Memories of the Future*).

3

EvD of plagiarism, and questions many of his hypotheses. As the chief opponent of the ascendant Swiss author, has been given the title 'Anti-Däniken'. Wrote his polemic at the age of eighteen, while a student at the Free University of Berlin. Appeared against EvD in several public debates. However, considers their thematic differences set apart from their personal relationship. At EvD's invitation, Gadow spent several weeks with him in the United States in autumn of 1974. He is single and lives in West Berlin.

HANS NEUNER: Austrian, 33. Lessee of a restaurant in the Tyrolean tourist centre Leutasch, near Seefeld. Completed an extensive education in the culinary arts. Met and was befriended by EvD in Davos. Accompanied Däniken on his first expedition. Is married, has a son and a daughter.

WILHELM UTERMANN: German, 65. Nicknamed 'Utz'. Married, three sons. Accomplished in every literary field. Has been both a journalist and a scriptwriter. Has written plays and novels, and produced several successful films, among them *The Trapp Family* and *The Black Sheep*, which starred Heinz Rühmann. His more than thirty-year acquaintanceship with publisher Erwin Barth von Wehrenalp led in 1967 to his being offered the task of rewriting the raw first manuscript of a certain Erich von Däniken. From this early professional association with EvD a genuine friendship developed. In Däniken's books Utermann appears as Wilhelm Roggersdorf, his editorial pen-name. Roggersdorf is the name of the town where he lives, in Upper Bavaria.

ERWIN BARTH VON WEHRENALP: Part-German (he says Prussian), part-Austrian, 65. Co-founder in 1950 of the publishing house ECON. Today ECON is one of the largest publishers of non-fiction in the German speaking countries. Well-known writers are published by ECON: Werner Keller, *Und die Bibel hat doch Recht* (*And Indeed the Bible was Right*), Rudolf Pörtner, *Mit dem Fahrstuhl in die Römerzeit* (*To the Roman Era by Elevator*), and Johannes Lehmann, *Jesus-Report*. But Erich von Däniken holds the top position in Wehrenalp's stable of authors. More than 37 million copies of his books—translated into 33 languages—have been sold throughout the world. Still, in 1967 it required a shove by *Dr Zeit* editor Thomas von Randow before the then sceptical ECON publisher was moved to print von Däniken's first book.

The writer of this book also has a word or two of his own to say in the following pages:

4

PETER KRASSA: Austrian, 38. Previously a bank employee, then a journalist. Now a free-lance writer. Entered the literary field as the author of speculative non-fiction—1973, *Als die Gelben Götter Kamen* (*When the Yellow Gods Came*);1974, *Gott Kam von den Sternen* (*God Came from the Stars*). Has enjoyed mutual friendship with EvD for many years; they made an American tour together in 1974. Single, lives in Vienna. Here in his third book has resolved to portray Erich von Däniken with 'benevolent criticism'.

So much for the personnel. The book contains the sum total of all they know about Däniken. It describes EvD's characteristics frankly, in all their colourful multiplicity.

The portrait of an iridescent personality. As he really exists, as no individual person knows him. After all, the title is: *The Intimate Däniken*.

One of the twelve of us hit on a definition of the Swiss *enfant terrible* which seems to me about as close as you can get to defining EvD. Eduardo Chaves said, 'Only a very, very few like him exist. How can one even begin to describe him? I know of no better way than: Erich von Däniken is simply—Erich von Däniken.'

I hope that you too come to know him through this book!

Vienna, March 1976   PETER KRASSA

CHAPTER I

For and Against

Is Erich von Däniken at the end of the road? Are his fantastic theories only delusions? Such heretical suggestions were rife in the mass media in the summer of 1975, after the apparent miscarriage of an expedition to Kashmir led by the Swiss god-seeker.

Equipped with a fully-outfitted Range Rover and £40,000 worth of equipment, EvD and his secretary and closest co-worker Willi Dünnenberger set out for Pakistan that August. He sought final and irrefutable proof of his theory—that intelligent extra-terrestrial beings had once visited this planet and had left traces of their presence at certain locations. It appeared that there might be such a 'certain location' in the Vale of Kashmir, at a Semitic temple near Srinagar.

An ancient historian and German school principal, Karl Maier, had thrown Däniken a hint. He drew upon an Old Testament episode which reported that the prophet Ezekiel, after his first meeting with extra-terrestrial visitors, was flown by them to an unknown temple, one obviously outside Palestine.

On the basis of relatively detailed descriptions in the Biblical text, Dr Maier homed in on a ruined temple in the Vale of Kashmir, although it was known that this temple, near Srinagar, was erected in the eighth century AD. According to the data in the prophet's book, Ezekiel's flight took place in 573 BC.

Nevertheless, Däniken didn't let this stop him from following up the clue, for he thought it possible that the later temple could have been built upon the ruins of an earlier tabernacle. With the aid of Geiger counters he was going to try to verify whether radioactive traces could still be detected in the temple area. He was also encouraged by the fact that there were corroborative, though vague, indications of the temple elsewhere in the Biblical text.

6

Returning from an exhaustive and exhausting tour of the Srinagar temple, a greatly-disappointed Däniken announced to press representatives in New Delhi: 'I found no confirmation of the Biblical account. The temple could not have been at the stated location.'

Were there therefore, no traces of ancient astronauts in Kashmir? Was the search entirely fruitless?

Let us leave that question for the moment, and ask about Däniken's report of his expedition to Ecuador. This had raised a storm of controversy, especially in German-speaking countries, when in his third book, *Aussaat und Kosmos*, EvD optimistically stated:

> To me this is the most incredible, the most improbable story of the century.
>
> It could be a science-fiction story, if I myself had not seen and photographed the unbelievable. What I have seen is neither dream nor fantasy, it is reality. . . .

What he claimed to have seen was an extensive tunnel-system, meandering for a distance of several thousand kilometres deep in the earth between Peru and Ecuador. He himself had been down there, maintained Däniken obstinately, together with the true discoverer of these artificially excavated caves and corridors, Juan Moricz, an Argentinian of Hungarian descent.

Moricz had already spied out these subterranean passages in 1965, but had concealed his discovery for the next three years. Then in 1969 he set out for the tunnels once again with a seventeen-man party. However, various troubles—tropical rainfall, shortage of provisions —beset the expedition, and the undertaking miscarried.

Moricz and Däniken met for the first time on March 4, 1972. After an hour-long conversation, the distrustful Argentinian was persuaded to show the Swiss god-seeker his secret. He led Däniken and his companion, Franz Seiner, to a side entrance of the tunnel complex. This was located in the Ecuadorean province of Santiago-Zamora, within the triangle Gualaquiza–San Antonio–Yaupi; the area is inhabited by hostile Indians. Moricz withheld more specific details from Däniken.

No matter—Erich von Däniken found himself at his goal. The proof of his conviction, that Lords from other stars had once been here, was clearly visible all around him. In awe, he wrote:

> The tunnel walls are velvety, and accurately plumbed; sometimes narrow, sometimes wide. Some walls are smooth as if they had been polished, the floor level and slick as if coated with glaze.

7

These corridors surely did not originate from natural causes—modern air-raid shelters have interiors like these!

Von Däniken was fascinated—then surprise piled on surprise. First his compass broke down. Moricz explained that this was supposedly due to radiation. Then, suddenly, he saw a skeleton lying on the ground before him, powdered with gold-dust. 'As if from a spray-can,' he thought.

They proceeded further, and entered a hall whose floor area EvD estimated to be 110 by 130 metres. He compared the dimensions with those of Teotihuacan's Pyramid of the Sun. Here as with the Pyramid, the ingenious constructors, the superb technicians of the building, remained anonymous.

The hall was not empty. It contained a table and seven chairs but of what material—stone, wood, metal?—Däniken didn't know. The surfaces of the familiar objects felt to him 'like self-annealed plastic'; but they were heavy and hard as steel.

Animals stood behind the chairs; lizards, elephants, lions, crocodiles, jaguars, camels, bears, apes, bison, wolves, crawling lizards, snails, crayfish. They were not displayed in pairs like the animals in Noah's Ark; nor as zoologists prefer, according to class and genus; nor in a way biologists would recognise, in natural evolutionary sequence.

'It is a zoological garden of *madness*, and its animals are made of pure *gold.* . . .' The two words in italic in the sentence, would lead later to a verbal fusillade against Däniken.

Of course his *report* was mad, and untrue; this story about the underground caverns; his description of the golden treasures to be found there was a lie. That was the judgment of many scientists and journalists. And various German opinion-mongers maliciously brushed aside EvD's most sensational disclosure—that in another hall 'opposite the zoological garden, to the left behind the conference table' he had paused to inspect a library of *metal plates*!

Partly plates, partly millimetre-thin metal foil, most of them about 48 by 96 centimetres. After long critical consideration, it is inexplicable to me what material could have a consistency making it possible for such large, thin foil-like sheets of it to remain upright. They stand next to one another like pages bound into giant volumes. Each sheet is lettered, bears impressions, is uniform as if printed by machine. Moricz has never counted the pages in his metal library; I accept his estimate that there could be several thousand. . . .

Deposited with the public notary Gustavo Falconi in Guayaquil there is a legally-verified document signed by Juan Moricz and several witnesses, in which the Ecuadorean Government and the other parties concerned legitimise his role as the discoverer of the mysterious tunnel complex (EvD has a photocopy of this document, dated July 21, 1969). In an interview which appeared in *Der Spiegel* in 1973, Moricz gave another version of Däniken's visit.

The Argentinian asserted that Däniken had never been in his tunnels. His Swiss guest likewise had not seen the metal library nor the golden zoo with his own eyes. To the astounded *Spiegel* reporter's question: what had led Däniken to make such statements, Moricz replied testily:

I *told* him everything. For hours, for days, he squeezed me dry. Always he wanted to hear more. He even hinted at the sum of $200,000 for an expedition to explore the caverns. . . .

Indeed, Däniken was actually at a side entrance to the labyrinth.

. . . But one cannot enter the system at this spot, the passage is obstructed. Däniken can lie as much as he wishes, but not I. . . .

So—had Däniken really lied? Did Juan Moricz speak the truth? The god-seeker countered vehemently. 'If Moricz and I were merely at a side-entrance at which, so he says, "there was nothing to see", why should he have led me there at all? Why did we have to trek for 48 hours by jeep and on foot through the primeval forest? Only to succeed in reaching an entrance which was supposedly blocked, and where "there was nothing to see"?'

Even *Der Spiegel* didn't present Mr Moricz as being a very reliable character. The director of the Quito Archaeological Institute, Hernan Crespo Toral, called him bluntly a 'swindler and adventurer'. And *Der Spiegel* was convinced that neither Moricz nor Däniken had ever seen the golden zoo or the metal library. '. . . but unlike Däniken, Moricz probably never really believed in their existence.'

Certainly, the legend of the golden zoo and the other artifacts to be found in the Ecuadorean caverns has been current in the area for a long time. An allegedly insane Captain Jaramillo reported on the subject forty years ago.

This means that neither Däniken nor Moricz necessarily lied. And as we soon will see, the *Spiegel* investigator treated the matter too flippantly. After all, that notarised affidavit of the Argentinian cave-explorer still exists, and it is also a fact that in 1969 a seventeen-man group which included Moricz took part in such an expedition. They drove through to the tunnel-system's main entrance. A great many photographs were taken on this trip. The men *were* in the caverns, verified their artificial origin, and saw with their own eyes artifacts placed there in long past millennia. Because of various adverse circumstances the expedition was not completed as planned, and Juan Moricz had the entire team sign a document in which they swore secrecy about all they had seen and experienced. Photocopies of this paper exist.

And finally, there is support in the form of correspondence from the American film company Media Associates, which takes an unequivocal position with regard to the existence of this mysterious tunnel-complex. The author of this book has read the written evidence.

On March 5, 1973, EvD received the first of a series of letters from the director of the film company, James B. Mobley. He informed the Swiss that negotiations with Moricz had been broken off. The Hungarian exile had initially been ready to guide the film team through his caverns in return for a principal sum of $50,000 plus $1000 per expedition. Then he suddenly changed his mind, and declared that he would agree only to a filmed interview. The film company rejected this offer.

However, Media Associates adapted quickly to this setback. They dismissed Moricz, searched for and found a new guide for the expedition, one Pino Torrola. Däniken learned that Torrola 'had explored the caves more thoroughly than any other person, at least 18 months before the Moricz expedition. . . .' EvD was overjoyed—finally, a gleam of light on the cloudy horizon, and the possibility of being able to support his *Aussaat und Kosmos* assertions with filmed proof. Director Mobley wrote to him:

After extensive investigation we have come to the conclusion that if there are machines, plates of strange metal, golden articles, etcetera, to be found in the caves, they will not be found within those chambers visited by Mr Moricz but in certain other chambers many miles distant, beneath the upper course of the Santiago River. The entrance is accessible only by swimming underwater and emerging inside the caves. Our expedition will investigate both sets of chambers, those of Mr Moricz and those at the river. If there is any basis at all for these tales, we have ample opportunity to determine what is and what is not true. One thing is certain: We'll make this film into a great adventure.

EvD wrote again to Moricz' attorney, Mattheus Pena. In an earlier letter Pena had requested for his client a percentage of the proceeds from von Däniken's books, because EvD had—illegally, it was asserted—publicised the discovery of the Argentinian spelaeologist. The letter also included a reference to plagiarism of the substance of Moricz' ideas. Däniken countered:

A percentage share of my works to date is out of the question. Ideas and theories can not be patented; no one has a ghost of a claim to them. I have already written to you concerning the pictures I had published. In Mr Seiner's presence, Mr Moricz released these few photographs for publication.

Additionally, a reprimand is in order here because of the fact that these pictures had already been published *before* I ever obtained them from Mr Moricz.... I find it extraordinarily unjust to encourage me while in Ecuador to report on Mr Moricz' subterranean complex, and then—after this is done—to suddenly about-face. Indeed, it was the object and purpose of our conversations, and it was my task, to inform the world that Mr Moricz had discovered underground caves and a treasure chamber. It was intended to call the attention of the outside world to Mr Moricz. As far as I'm concerned, this is what has occurred. To now demand royalty payments from me—royalties for what?—is a joke.

While he was about it, EvD also set the record straight about Moricz' assertion in *Der Spiegel* that he had promised the Argentinian $200,000 for a cave-expedition.

I repeat once more that it's entirely accurate that I assured Moricz in our conversations that I would bend my endeavours toward raising the backing for an expedition. We had discussed how a large firm—or several of them—could share expenses in order to make such an expedition possible. These firms would receive some sort of advertising or publicity rights in return. Our friendly dialogues were along these lines, without ever settling on definite arrangements or drawing up contracts.... Now as before, I'm convinced that it would be possible to raise large sums for a Juan Moricz expedition, as long as Mr Moricz makes binding pledges to the companies concerned. For logically, nobody is going to make a present of $200,000 without an assurance of some equivalent value in return. Will you be so kind as to inform me, in return for *which* equivalent value am I supposed to have promised this alleged $200,000?

Attorney Pena did not deign to reply; he did not remain idle, however, for Däniken had of course informed him that Media Associates 'now intend to exploit the Ecuadorean caverns cinematographically, independent of Mr Moricz'. The justifiably exasperated Swiss also mentioned that one-and-a-half years earlier a certain Pino Torrola had visited the caverns and was now to guide the American film team to them. And this was to have unfortunate results, as was shown by subsequent events.

In the autumn of 1973, Däniken showed me a further communication from Director Mobley, one which, understandably, filled him with a sense of achievement. Torrola and the cinema crew had been in the caverns and had exposed several thousand metres of film. After difficult manoeuvres—forced jungle-marches and diving operations before the cave entrance could be reached—it had at last been possible to let the cameras roll 'We filmed in halls of undoubtedly artificial origin, halls in which 6000 persons could easily have found room,' enthused Mobley. Instead of a documentary, it was intended to make a dramatic film from the footage; in a couple of months Däniken would receive the results of these endeavours, and could see for himself.

I well remember the joy with which EvD sent or handed me each letter as it arrived. It was all so clear to him: in a few months his theories and statements, held in such disdain in professional circles and by the news media, would receive glorious cinematographic confirmation.

But Däniken's editor, Utz Utermann, had already begun to have doubts. 'I asked a good friend of mine in Hollywood to try to attend the rushes,' he reminisced. 'My friend endeavoured to, but with no success. The film just never surfaced.'

What had happened? Utermann reasoned it out logically. 'Look, according to Ecuadorean law, any discoveries made in that country belong to the discoverer; no part of them may be removed or exported. But that was certainly not the intention of the film team, so there must be *something* there that we—including the zealous reporters—are not supposed to know about. Däniken was threatened with an uninterrupted series of lawsuits in Ecuador, court actions such as he's never had before anywhere in the world. Not even in other South American countries, where *Aussaat und Kosmos* has long been a bestseller.'

To Utermann it was perfectly obvious, not only that Moricz and his group wanted to supplement their earnings from the sales of Däniken's book, but that they were playing with marked cards which, he was convinced, 'would one day be laid out flat on the table'. Not until then would Erich von Däniken be fully vindicated.

Had the Swiss god-seeker also practised a little deception, or were his descriptions based on fact? Why hadn't he kept track of the Americans' 'vanished' film himself? Had he invented the whole story? Did his knowledge of the tunnel-system rest solely on the reports of its discoverer?

ECON Publications was interested in shedding light on the whole mysterious tale. To that end in the spring of 1973 Erwin Barth von Wehrenalp financed an expedition to Ecuador by the well-known Bonn ethnologist Udo Oberem. But the undertaking didn't go according to plan. Utermann described some of the obstacles in Oberem's path: 'For instance, the spot from which the cave entrance is accessible may be reached only by air. Professor Oberem did indeed locate a plane after prolonged efforts—but the pilot who should have flown it to the vicinity of the entrance had long before returned to Argentina, for lack of flight assignments. There was no other way of reaching the caves; the rainy season was on, and floods were everywhere. It would have been idiotic to try to make it with a jeep—one would have gotten permanently stuck in the mud.'

'And if Däniken had taken it upon himself. . . .?' Utermann shook his head. 'Erich had the impulse to return immediately to Ecuador. I advised and implored against it, as did all who had influence with him. Look: both Juan Moricz and his attorney Pena are well accredited Ecuadorean citizens. What if they'd pulled strings to have Erich arrested right at the border? Believe me, there are all sorts of shady goings-on in Ecuador. Moricz told Erich about the caves, and guided him there through a side-access. But he said not a word concerning remuneration if Erich should write a report about it. On the contrary—I'm familiar with the correspondence. Indeed, if Moricz wanted to be paid for his representations, he should have said, "Mr von Däniken, if you write about this trip it will cost you, say, ten thousand dollars." Then Erich could have thought it over. And as I know him, he would have certainly said "No!" *Aussaat und Kosmos* ran to 282 pages, and this account takes up scarcely fourteen; whether they were or were not included would not have affected the book's success.'

But here Utermann and I part company. And I'm not alone in holding a different opinion. These very same fourteen pages of the Ecuadorean adventure, so lightly-valued by Utermann, were a major reason for the heavy coverage Däniken's third book received in the mass media, a fact acknowledged by EvD himself. Utermann complains about negative reviews, like those which appeared in the magazines *Spiegel* and *Stern*. He believes such reviews damaged the success of *Aussaat und Kosmos* in German-speaking countries. Both he and von Wehrenalp are convinced that the god-seeker is speaking the truth. Utermann quotes Däniken's companion Franz Seiner, who accompanied him as photographer. To Utermann's initial doubts about what had really happened in Ecuador and whether the story of the visit to the subterranean caverns was true, Seiner retorted heatedly, 'I'm surely not crazy! I was there with Erich, I went with him into the side entry—and Erich has never asserted otherwise. If Erich is insane, am I too? Two madmen, simultaneously but only temporarily? That would really be insanity!'

And ECON-chief, von Wehrenalp, cannot find a trace of anything wrong in EvD's story either: 'I am absolutely convinced that Erich von Däniken was where he said he was. But a certain rivalry seems to exist between Moricz and Däniken. I have the feeling that in this instance Däniken placed more trust in a person than he should have.'

The writer, Walter Ernsting, a prolific author of science fiction under the pen-name Clark Darlton, has been numbered among the Däniken 'insiders' for the past nine years. He entertains not the slightest doubt as to the Swiss's veracity. 'It's a fact that even before Erich travelled to Ecuador, a report was published in the magazine *Bild der Wissenschaft* about artificially-excavated tunnels in Peru. This report was written by recognised scientists—and reads even more fantastically than does von Däniken's. But no one got stirred up over it then. It was read, noted and forgotten.'

Ernsting accepts Däniken's description of the Ecuadorean caverns in its entirety, with the slight reservation: 'Perhaps as regards certain details Erich let his imagination run away with him.' But by no means, says Ernsting, has Däniken 'knowingly lied'. Like Wehrenalp, he sees his friend taken in by Juan Moricz. Nevertheless, 'Däniken saw what he said he saw, of that I am convinced!'

Ernsting awarded the best-selling author a metaphorical bouquet of roses, thorns and all: 'It seems to be Erich's fate to be taken even more seriously than eminent scientists. In any case, he certainly has more critics than they do.' The 57-year-old author of the world-renowned space series *Perry Rhodan* feels a special sympathy for his friend with regard to critics. Vehemently, with the touchiness of one who himself has often been unjustly attacked, he stands by EvD. 'It seems to me that many reporters and critics hold the view that whatever crosses their path—no matter whether it's a film, a book or an actor—can be dealt with solely by negative criticism. Apparently they're of the opinion that only then can the subject be taken seriously. They believe that praise would be regarded as a sign of weakness.'

Erich von Däniken's excursions to Kashmir and Ecuador were only two of numerous exploratory expeditions in search of proof of his theories. Save the People's Republic of China and the Soviet Union (except for Moscow), there isn't one significant nation on earth he hasn't combed through, trying to add still more material to his accumulation of circumstantial evidence that Earth was visited by 'Gods' in remote prehistory. The binding of this book would split if all the trips of the Swiss 'mischief-maker' were to be cited in chronological order. Also many details of his travels and experiences are known only to his close associates.

But Erich von Däniken searches further, for the final link in his chain of evidence: *the* proof. On occasion, when queried by curious fans or reporters, he speaks vaguely of a 'mathematically-logical point somewhere in our solar system', without abandoning the hope that eventually it will be discovered in the solid ground beneath his feet. I am also of the opinion that the Swiss seeker-after-gods speaks the truth concerning his Ecuador adventure. Certainly, in detailed accounts related only to his closest friends there are facts which others besides EvD would consider as authentic evidence.

I am not entirely content with the ostensible reasons for Däniken's stubborn refusal to undertake another visit to Ecuador. It's true that he has been warned repeatedly that he may again fall victim to the machinations of Juan Moricz, dampening his original determination to thread his way once more through the tunnels which lead to the library of metal-foil volumes. Were it only a matter of this collection of books printed in mysterious characters, I could understand his stubbornness—although they would be evidence indeed! But in that subterranean labyrinth, says Däniken, he discovered a *thing*, an essence, an emotional perception, if you will, that—if he speaks sincerely—must be recognised and accepted as *the* proof.

His justification, 'I saw it, I felt it—it makes no difference to me what others believe!' is therefore unconvincing; for EvD—everyone who knows him will agree—lets no obstacle stand in his path to the goal of his life as an investigator: the Final Proof! He himself is the living confirmation of his own conviction of the identity of extra-terrestrial astronauts.

So—two conclusions may be drawn as to the motives for Däniken's refusal to return to the Ecuadorean caves, the site of his discovery:

— Either the god-seeker *lied*, and his 'evidence' was a pure invention;
— Or there is some source of danger in Ecuador which exceeds every conjecture about it, something so frightful that it can deter even one as determined as Däniken from attaining his final goal.

Then must the Swiss traveller always tot up a negative balance sheet? Failure all along the line, in Ecuador as in Kashmir?

This question needs some modification.

Kashmir was not a failure, Däniken made sure that every setback was faithfully reported by the media. And why?

It is well known that relations between India and Pakistan are strained. They have no diplomatic relations; all necessary diplomatic contact is maintained through neutral Switzerland. Consequently, crossing the border between India and Pakistan is even now a minor adventure. Natives of the two countries avoid the frontier. Most of those who cross over are foreigners, perhaps an average of ten per day at each official station.

Erich von Däniken's 'expedition' consisted of only two members, himself and his secretary Willi Dünnenberger. Certainly the quantity of luggage was sufficient for an entire company of assault troops. In the crammed Range Rover there were not only fifteen bags and cases, but also various instruments such as radiation probes, metal detectors, typewriters, dictation units, photo apparatus and of course weapons—gas pistols. One must be armed against any eventuality on such a long journey.

Even against the police, both regular and clandestine.

EvD had taken much of his equipment with him illegally. The fact that nothing came of it can be laid to customs. Von Däniken: 'Thank God, most of the customs officials on the Pakistan–India border are illiterate. Their understanding is absolutely nil. You can even hand over your passport upside-down—they'll say "okay" and stamp it. On the other hand, their lack of education can lead to horrible complications. For instance, one of them may suspect a simple radio of being an item of secret-police equipment.' But if EvD had identified all his instruments truthfully, his expedition would have foundered before it began. 'If the customs officers had discovered that I had radiation-and metal-detectors in my gear, the expedition would have survived for perhaps six weeks, of that I'm convinced. The bewildered officials would have turned me over to the Indian Secret Service, and a series of hearings would have ensued. So we said nothing, and if a customs officer looked suspiciously at a Geiger counter, we declared barefacedly that it was a radio receiver.'

If some mistrustful officer requested that the apparatus be demonstrated, the Swiss duo were not unprepared. Däniken: 'We'd set the Geiger counter to tick off background radiation, and simply tell the customs man that there must be some atmospheric interference with radio reception.'

Customs eventually accepted every white lie that Däniken proffered—the way to the temple near Srinagar was open.

After Däniken's return to the Kashmir capital from the temple site, he gave a lecture at the local university, in an auditorium filled to overflowing. Again his theme was the gods-as-astronauts theory, and as usual there was a question-and-answer period. But Indian journalists had heard rumours about Däniken's projected visit to the temple ruins, and asked him curiously what he had found there. Däniken: 'I couldn't reveal to these good people that I'd been looking for traces of radioactivity in the temple area. They would have immediately asked, "With what equipment?"'

Due to the state of war-readiness between India and Pakistan, and Indira Gandhi's dictatorship at that time, India was mistrustful of strangers. The secret police had agents everywhere—people were denouncing their neighbours. EvD had to keep silent in order to avoid time-consuming difficulties. Therefore he described his search as fruitless. 'No, we found nothing,' he stated sorrowfully to the expectant journalists. He had found nothing finer in India than the surroundings, the pleasant people and the good food.

But even that was a lie. 'For the people weren't pleasant, and the food was terrible,' said Däniken, setting the record straight.

However, the adventurous trip to the mysterious shrine 80 kilometres beyond Srinagar—called locally the Sun- or Hebrew-temple— was not in vain. It revealed exciting indications, and a *de facto* confirmation of Biblical text.

The prophet Ezekiel had written the truth—Headmaster Maier's conjectures had finally been proved right. How so?

In the Old Testament is found the extremely interesting Book of Ezekiel. Together with a group of leading Jews, the Israelite priest and prophet was deported to a spot near Babylon in 597 BC. This was shortly after Jerusalem had fallen to Nebuchadnezzar, King of Babylon.

In his writings Ezekiel described his wondrous experiences with beings from the Cosmos, whose landing vehicle, the 'Glory of the Lord' he first encountered in spring of 593 BC. These encounters were repeated on three further occasions spread over the ensuing twenty years. Ezekiel's first rendezvous took place on the River Chebar at Tel-Abib near Babylon, where the deportees made their home. The priest, a clever and discerning man, was singled out by the space-travellers to transmit their instructions to his companions—which he did.

So Ezekiel was a witness to the 'Divine Spectacle'. The strangers took him into their spaceship and transported him first to Solomon's temple in Jerusalem, and later to a then-unfamiliar sanctum on a high mountain near a city.

NASA-engineer Josef Blumrich soon concluded from his researches that this second temple could *not* have been located in the Holy Land, that on no account was Solomon's Temple being referred to. Records exist of the floor-plan and appearance of the latter.

The detailed and exact description of the unknown temple in the Book of Ezekiel allows of no other conclusion: the prophet was flown by the strangers to the grounds about another temple, located outside the country.

But where should one search for it? Headmaster Karl Maier found a helpful clue. It led him, with the aid of atlas and travel-guide, to the Indian province (Jammu and) Kashmir, and its capital, Srinagar.

Srinagar had not always been Kashmir's metropolis. The earlier capital was called Martand. Its ruins lie a few hours distant from Srinagar, upstream along the Jhelum River. Close by are the remains of the former Hebrew temple, which remains today as an archaeological riddle.

Srinagar is at an altitude of 1600 metres (5200 feet), in the broad centre of the Jhelum River valley, surrounded by some of the tallest Himalayan giants. These peaks reach heights of four to six thousand metres (13,000 to 20,000 feet). But in the pertinent passage in the Book of Ezekiel, he says, 'In the visions of God brought he me into the land of Israel, and set me upon a very high mountain, by which was as the frame of a city on the south.' (40,2)

Engineer Blumrich as well as headmaster Maier are positive that Ezekiel could not have been in the Holy Land at that time, for Jerusalem and its surroundings would have been as familiar to him 'as his own vest-pocket', and he would certainly have known the name of the 'very high mountain'. No, the area to which he had been brought was obviously unknown to him.

Maier avers that in this region (Kashmir) there are numerous recognisable links with Hebrew tradition. There are towns, for example, which even today bear the names of Biblical cities; one sees women in typical Jewish costume, and notes Hebrew characters incised on gravestones. Many family names are suffixed with the particle -*yu* or -*ju*, and other similar indications abound.

Erich von Däniken, as is his wont, wished to know the facts in detail. So he set out upon the search for the Hebrew temple of Srinagar. 'We visited about 25 such temples in Kashmir, all of them shrines dedicated to Hindu divinities. Only this one temple near Srinagar did not match the others,' stated EvD. The layout of the temple and the temple grounds corresponded in detail to Ezekiel's report. Also, it wasn't actually near Srinagar, but near the ruins of the former metropolis Martand. Däniken: 'In fact, the structure was quite extensive, built in a fashion similar to that of Solomon's Temple in Jerusalem, whose plans have survived until today. Unfortunately, the temple itself was destroyed in 586 BC, seven years after Ezekiel's first contact with the space-travellers.'

But what was Däniken really looking for? We refer again to the Bible. There are hints in Ezekiel's written account that in the other temple, the one presumed to be in Kashmir, radioactive material may be buried. It is stated, for example:

> And he spake unto the man clothed with linen, and said, Go in between the wheels, even under the cherub, and fill thine hand with coals of fire from between the cherubims. . . . (10,2)
> . . . then he went in, and stood beside the wheels. And one cherub stretched forth his hand from between the cherubims unto the fire that was between the cherubims, and took thereof, and put it into the hands of him that was clothed with linen; who took it, and went out. (10,6,7)

Certainly, 'glowing coals' doesn't refer to any common fuel known to us—evidently something more significant is being described.

Erich von Däniken and his assistant Willi Dünnenberger carried on an intensive search for radiation over several days. They covered not only the area within the temple proper, but also the temple's four portals. EvD deduced with good reason that the space-travellers could have left radioactive traces behind them as they entered the temple. In the words of Ezekiel:

> Afterward he brought me to the gate, even the gate that looketh toward the east. (43,1)
> And behold, the glory of the God of Israel came from the way of the east, and his voice was like a noise of many waters: and the earth shined with his glory. (43,2)
> And it was according to the appearance of the vision which I saw, even according to the vision that I saw when he came to destroy the city; and the visions were like the vision that I saw by the river Chebar: and I fell upon my face. (43,3)
> And the glory of the Lord came into the house, by the way of the gate whose prospect is toward the east. (43,4)

In his book *The Spaceships of Ezekiel*, Josef Blumrich, sounding out the bases of Ezekiel's writings with his usual scientific thoroughness, unwittingly lent ammunition to von Däniken. The god-seeker *did* come upon a radioactive trace. Not by the east portal, however, but at the *north* portal of the temple. Däniken: 'The radiation detector we had was of extraordinary sensitivity. We could have picked up radioactive traces left 250 centuries ago, not just a mere twenty-five. It was an altogether fantastic instrument, with almost limitless possibilities. For instance, it could be set to detect and discriminate between alpha, beta or gamma rays, or any rays at all. Then if it started to crackle, you could sort them out: "what type of rays are being indicated?"' EvD and his young companion were affected with discovery-fever. Their hope that the temple's secret would be revealed was probably far greater than their confidence. Then this occurred:

'We had already covered part of the temple area with our Geiger counter, at first in vain. We had just crossed the extended line of the main (north) portal when we were suddenly startled by a fearful racket in the phones, and the counter's needle vibrating crazily. The sound was like the stutter of a machine-gun. For a moment I thought we'd heard wrongly, and disbelieving such a discovery, retraced my steps the entire way. Repeat. It was no error; the loud crackling came again. Here was a spot of increased radioactivity. It was at such a high level that we couldn't measure it, higher than the full scale of our instrument; the needle seemed as if it were trying to escape.' EvD frantically pressed and turned all the control knobs, trying to find one that would moderate the deafening racket. In vain— the noise in both sets of headphones remained constant.

Däniken: 'That was a curious thing—our measurements showed a radioactive strip just one-and-a-half metres wide. Outside this band our instrument was silent, but as soon as we crossed into it the fearful rattle began again—rat-tat-tat-tat-ta.'

Now they tried to measure the length of this ribbon of radio-activity. 'Our 25-metre tape measure marked off exactly 52 metres (170 feet). Several boys had accompanied us, and we pressed them into service with a few coins to help us make the measurements accurately, lining them up along our course about three metres apart. As we took measurements and readings, we were gradually surrounded by children. One of us held the tape, the other the radiation counter. That was a wild occasion! And the wildest: the intensity remained at an unchanged level for the entire 52 metres. Through the main portal along a line straight as an arrow!'

EvD followed the radioactive trail left by the space-visitors within the temple. It led him—2500 years after their presumed first manifestation—straight to the temple's centre, a sacred shrine cruelly eroded by the ravages of time.

Däniken: 'At this central point was a massive monolith, a stone block which looked as if it had been poured, not hewn. It was about 2.8 metres on a side and one-and-a-half metres high, all of one piece. Even a crane would have had trouble moving the block from this spot. Our Geiger counter was unimpressed; it continued indicating clearly that the radiation-source was to be found in this stone mass. Underneath, perhaps, we didn't know. . . .'

However, Erich von Däniken still has hopes of finding answers to his questions. During his stay in India he was in constant touch with scholars at several universities. In contrast to his contacts with the press, he withheld nothing of the results of his explorations from these academics. He did this because these learned Indian professors had met his concepts with more open minds than had their European counter-parts. Däniken says: 'I've written them that I cannot explain the radioactivity in the temple. I begged them to follow up on my findings, perhaps make excavations there.'

So—we'll wait and see.

But how to explain the discrepancy between Ezekiel's reference to the temple's east portal and Däniken's findings at the *north* portal? I mentioned this to Josef Blumrich, who had encountered the same problem on his own. The NASA-expert believes he has found the most logical answer.

To recapitulate, the prophet Ezekiel was taken on several trips to a temple by spacecraft. He (or whichever Biblical scribe wrote the account) believed that it must have been Solomon's Temple in Jerusalem. But the accompanying description of the surroundings doesn't match nor does a reference to the outer forecourts. In this connection, Blumrich's book states:

> It is therefore quite interesting that Solomon's Temple ... had only *one* wall and no outer courts!... This surprising development is underscored by a discrepancy in the description of the terrain. In Chapter 9, Verse 2, we read that men 'came from the direction of the upper gate'. The above-mentioned map, on the other hand, shows the building of the temple on a hill; the north gate of the temple of Solomon was therefore situated *lower*.

The conclusion remains that Ezekiel was not in Solomon's Temple at all—that his temple excursions had taken him to that shrine near Martand, with no inkling of where or what it was.

After all, even the Biblical commentator isn't really sure in what direction lay the gate through which passed the 'Glory of God'. Quoting Blumrich: '... so that, in the final analysis, the location of the gate still remains in doubt.' As a further indication of the accuracy of his supposition, that Ezekiel's landfall was in Kashmir rather than in Israel, the modern Bible-commentator from NASA offers the priest's remark that it took place 'upon the mountain which is on the east side of the city'.

Adduces Blumrich incisively: 'Someone who knew Jerusalem as well as Ezekiel did would not only as a matter of course know the name of that mountain—the one we call the Mount of Olives—but would certainly have used this familiar name in an equally matter-of-fact way had he really wanted to refer to that mountain, especially in speaking to people who like himself were perfectly familiar with the area. We remember in this connection that Ezekiel never fails to mention his community of exiles "by the river Chebar".'

Blumrich also considers the fact—this seems especially worth noting —that the Book of Ezekiel in the form handed down to us is not a first-person report of the Israelite priest himself.

Blumrich: 'An editor of Ezekiel's Book could therefore in good faith and with the best intentions have seen the temple of this encounter in the general religious context, and could have placed it in Jerusalem.'

I draw upon a significant detail from the 1959 edition of the *Lexicon für Theologie und Kirche* which may or may not have bearing in this connection. There it says: 'Later (generations of) Jews forbade the reading of (Ezekiel's) first and last chapters, because of their obscurity.' Not surprising: just those excerpts from the beginning and ending of the Book of Ezekiel describe the contacts between extra-terrestrials and the Israelite priest. Strict Talmudic scholars wanted nothing to do with Ezekiel's fantasy-tinged reports.

But we, children on the threshold of the third millennium, can see more clearly. Surely this is due in appreciable measure to the perceptions of a Blumrich, a Maier or a Däniken. The accumulation of evidence increases continually.

So, to repeat the initial question—is Erich von Däniken at the end of the road? The answer may sound blasphemous to many: No, by God! Not even one-hundredth of the earth's surface has been explored archaeologically; is there still anyone who can honestly maintain that there is nothing new to be discovered?

And as for the 'Ecuadorean controversy', take my word for it, the last word on that has not yet been spoken. Wealthy firms and institutions are queuing up behind Däniken—they all stand ready with financial support for an expedition to the mysterious cave-world of Ecuador. EvD gives any such undertaking his blessing, with one restriction: he himself does not want to go there again. It is too risky for him.

Däniken's personal misgivings are certainly not groundless. A news item appeared in January 1976 with the information that the balance of power had recently been altered. The man who governed as president until then, Lara, was forced to yield his position to a three-man military junta. Such unrest discolours 'the native hue of resolution'.

Postscript: In July 1976 an international hundred-man expedition initiated by Scottish engineer Stanley Hall set out to delve into the mysteries of the caves of Ecuador The honorary chairman was a prominent person: Neil Armstrong, first man on the moon, now a professor at the University of Cincinnati. The joint British-Ecuadorean scientific teams are preparing reports which may take up to two years to complete, although a film and book for public release will probably appear sooner.

CHAPTER II

A Citizen of the World

Anyone who travels with Däniken, lives dangerously. Of course I never would have dreamed that that statement might have any relevance for me. But I became involved in a happening that under slightly different circumstances might have cost EvD his life.

This dramatic event occurred during the three-day Congress of the Ancient Astronaut Society held in Chicago in 1974. This fellowship, with over 2000 members worldwide, devotes itself to the task of finding and producing evidence that space-travellers visited this planet in ages past.

The most prominent guest at this first World Congress was Erich von Däniken. He, Walter Ernsting and I were the only European delegates; the largest number of scientists and writers was contributed by the United States. One delegation was from Japan. That danger would threaten us from that quarter came as a complete surprise.

The two- or three-man Japanese contingent (we were never sure of the number) had already taken rooms in the Arlington Park Towers before we arrived. They had set to work examining the list of participants and had immediately run up against the name *Erich von Däniken*. Minutes later they requested an interview with attorney Gene Phillips, founder of the Society. He received the delegation in his office and listened to their demand with amazement; Däniken must leave! Phillips must withdraw his invitation at once. The Swiss was a wicked plagiarist—without authorisation, he had published photos of Japanese Dogu statuettes (remarkable bronze figures who appear to be wearing spacesuits) in his books, in defiance of copyright laws. The rights belonged to their Japanese UFO-group, growled the delegates indignantly, a fact which Däniken had simply ignored.

Gene Phillips was filled with consternation. The naked threat hung in the air, 'Either Däniken departs immediately, or something will happen. . . .' The lawyer knew at once that this was no bluff, but must be taken seriously. Yet he refused the Japanese demand. An offer to mediate a reconciliation between Däniken and the UFO-people was declined.

At this time Däniken, Ernsting and I knew nothing of the threatening clouds gathering in the astronauts' heavens. We had meanwhile taken our rooms, and what rooms! They were immense chambers where a game of Rugby could easily have been played. Shortly afterward we were warned; Phillips told us of the incident, his rejection of the Japanese demand and the first consequence: all the beautiful flower arrangements Japan had contributed for the Congress had been removed. What was going to happen?

We felt some trepidation upon meeting one of the Japanese in the corridor on the way to the conference-rooms. He recognised Däniken at once and his expression took on a threatening cast. Was it only his exotic appearance that affected me, or was he really dangerous?

Phillips took no chances. We met in Däniken's room and planned preventive measures. The attorney, Walter, myself and three conference assistants would 'shadow' Däniken incessantly.

For the first two days all was calm. Only one member of the Japanese group was in evidence. We kept him constantly in sight.

Then on the last day, April 28, it happened, during the slide-lecture given by our friend Josef Blumrich. The NASA engineer was presenting his version of the Ezekiel story, and as his lecture had been inconveniently scheduled for midday, the audience was sparse. Present were Däniken, Ernsting and I, Gene Phillips and the three society 'observers'. The Japanese was also there, apparently following Blumrich's lecture with interest.

Suddenly the lights in the hall went out. Chills ran up and down my spine. Was this the prelude to an assault on EvD? The other 'shadowers' probably thought as I did. Seconds later the lights came on again—but Däniken had disappeared. Had he been abducted? What was happening?

All eyes turned toward the Japanese. He still sat—apparently unconcerned—in the same place. And then we heaved a joint sigh of relief. Däniken was safe and sound. To be sure, he was sitting at the opposite end of the hall.

The reason for his move was clear; the Swiss was taking no chances. When the lights went out, he reacted quick as a flash, exchanging his seat for one at the opposite end of another row. Had an attack been attempted, the assailant would have had a problem—Däniken seemed to have dissolved into thin air.

The Congress proceeded without further incident. The power outage had not been artificially induced; it was an 'act of God'. Whatever it was that the Japanese intended, we never learned. The remaining hours passed without disturbance. Still—it had not been an altogether false alarm, of that I'm certain.

When someone feels a void in the pit of his stomach, he cannot afford to ignore it. I once felt such a void in the town of Florence, in the state of Alabama. Von Däniken had a stopover there, and Ernsting and I accompanied him. The lecture bureau of Erich's American publisher Bantam Books had arranged a fourteen-day lecture tour in April and May, taking in the Ancient Astronaut Congress. Florence was on the itinerary.

It is a typical American small town. Many religious sects flourish there, and it is only a slight exaggeration to say that almost every other building is a church. That would not have troubled us, but as a consequence it is illegal to sell liquor in Florence. Whoever wants to drink there must bring in his own alcohol from elsewhere.

We three knew nothing of this. That evening I accompanied EvD to his lecture. As almost everywhere in the USA, it was being presented at the local university. Every seat was occupied, and conspicuous in the audience were many members of the clergy.

During Däniken's talk I operated the slide projector. It was not located within the hall, as is customary, but in a space *behind* the lectern and the screen—a procedure called rear projection. Erich controlled the sequence of slides and my job was to change the slide tray at the proper time, which was not an especially difficult task. What was remarkable was that behind the stage where the projector stood, two policemen patrolled unceasingly back and forth, their thumbs hooked in their belts, Colt revolvers at the ready.

I don't know whether EvD on the rostrum realised what was going on, but there seemed to me to be an air of menace hovering above and about him. On no other occasion during that tour did I experience anything remotely similar.

A further twist to this curious affair revealed still more of the state of mind prevailing in the town of Florence. It is Däniken's habit to lighten his lectures with an occasional humorous aside. He spices his talks with a few harmless, though often risqué, witticisms. Always

26

with the same reaction: the audience is amused. This same banter was intended for Florence.

At the point where EvD reports about the Nazca Plains, and reflects on the origin of the huge figures scratched thereon (which can be seen only from the air), he usually mentions the possible initiators of the furrowed outlines—*priests*. 'Some priest had a brain-wave—' he often begins, setting up the next sentence: 'Indeed, priests always have good ideas.' This never fails to strike a spark, and Däniken always expects to hear a light ripple of laughter.

Not so in Florence. Scarcely had he let the punch-line fall when two persons—count them, two—began to laugh loudly, and kept it up for several seconds. At the height of their hilarity they broke it off sharply. The hall became silent as the tomb; the power of religion had triumphed. Afterwards, when the lecture was over, our own mood paralleled the silent disapproval of the Alabama Florentines.

At the hotel we were greeted by a bitter, stone-cold sober Walter Ernsting. How could such a thing have happened to him? To him, a moderate but daily imbiber. He had planned to prepare a marvellous midnight supper for Däniken and me, with wine and champagne. . . . Ridiculous! A couple of bottles of cola were all he could come up with.

Fuming, he turned in, while EvD and I sat up till morning talking shop. What luck! that Däniken now discovered a few souvenirs in his flight bag, in the form of miniature liquor bottles. We'd received them as favours from various airlines during our several domestic flights. Now we made use of them. Whisky and cola, just the thing to help us get rid of our irritation over bloody Florence. 'This hamlet will never see me again!' swore Däniken the next morning. I'll personally guarantee that oath will not be broken.

This American tour had more excitement in store for us. As long distances lay between lecture-stops, almost all of our travel was by air; we had to survive fifteen inland flights. There were no problems except for the flight by a light plane which we chartered to carry the three of us from Atlanta to Huntsville. Walter Ernsting remembers it with a faint shudder. As a science-fiction writer he knows how to tell the story best.

'Our first attempt to take off miscarried. The plane taxied to the end of the runway, the pilot gunned the engine—then he slacked off and taxied back to our original position. We sat there again in front of the terminal, rather at a loss. What had happened? We were informed that the machine was too heavy; some of the fuel was being drained. Then we rolled once more into take-off position. I, who always have a mild horror of flying anyway, felt even more faint than I usually do. Till now I've always trusted my guardian angel, and drawn comfort from the fact that my friend Däniken has been flying back and forth all over the world for years with no ill effects, no crashes. . . .

'So we started off again. The plane climbed steeply, the pilot evidently wanted to make up time he'd lost. We levelled off at a comparatively low altitude, for the Atlanta-Huntsville hop is a short one. But the pilot began to put the plane through some curious manoeuvres— first a sweeping curve to the left, then a precipitous turn right. Then an awkward sideslip. I threw a worried glance at Erich but got no reassurance; his face also exhibited a doubtful expression. He stared straight ahead, now and then taking a nip from his flask. Peter sat at the other window, gazing composedly out at the landscape as if nothing was happening. . . .'

Walter was mistaken; the word 'composed' in no way reflected my feelings! Why was I gazing so fixedly out the window? Try flying sometime next to a jet engine that's constantly *blubbering*. Something was wrong with the thing. I counted the minutes. Finally our landing field came in sight. Our pilot apparently still saw the need for haste, for we descended at the incline of a ski-slope. I snapped a quick glance at my companions and saw that they also were not unimpressed by these manoeuvres. They sat there pale of face. Finally, Ernsting was moved to ask, 'Erich, what have you learned from this crash course in flying?' Däniken, white around the gills: 'That our pilot must once have been a fighter pilot.' That's real humour, to be able to laugh through one's fears.

Other companions of the god-seeker have also survived flying adventures. One was Hans Neuner, who assisted EvD on three globe-trotting trips. The last of these ran from September through November of 1968, with Easter Island the ultimate destination.

'We started out from Chile, or more accurately, *intended* to start. Bad weather postponed our departure for several hours—we left at two am instead of nine the previous morning. The flight out was bearable, although the pilot had a little trouble finding the island. Mist and darkness hampered vision considerably.

'But the return flight was really an ordeal,' Neuner told me. 'After scarcely half-an-hour in the air, all the plane's windows became smeared with oil. One can imagine our alarm at this development.

Then the left engine conked out and the pilot shut it down. We were flying in a DC-9, an ancient model lacking every amenity. And now danger on top of discomfort. The pilot felt as insecure about continuing as we did, so we turned back.

'Easier said than done, for Easter Island now lay under thick cloud-cover. The pilot radioed the control tower. No answer. We soon knew why. Easter Island's Mataveri Airport is manned only during the infrequent landings and departures.

'Our pilot didn't give up, even though his spirits (and ours!) plunged. He transmitted steadily, but the control tower remained silent. Our uneasiness grew. From the cockpit came an announcement advising the passengers to fasten seat belts, which we did. We tried to blank our minds and disregard the facts: that we'd been circling above Easter Island for a long time, that we had no radio communication and that we'd better start making preparations for the inevitable splashdown.

'By sheer luck a couple of the ground crew finally became aware of the sound of our engines and alerted the tower personnel; with their aid we were able to set down through the fog, taking every precaution. We first learned the whole truth upon reaching solid ground: during the flight we had lost *two* of our four engines. It's amazing that we're alive today to tell the tale.'

After three hours wait while the engines were being repaired, Däniken and Neuner started out again for Chile. This time the flight went without incident. 'The Gods were on our side,' joked Hans Neuner. Eight years later he could still laugh about it.

'Laugh' is a key word, one which helps us to recall more clearly other episodes on our American trip. Like the one that occurred in the harbour city of Mobile, Alabama. We three were lodged in a charming bungalow-type hotel in a lovely park area on the edge of the city. There we experienced one of the most emotionally impressive evenings of the tour. Däniken, Ernsting and I spent this star-bright night sitting on the beach, languidly philosophising and enjoying the inactivity.

It had been the peace before the storm, which arrived on the following morning. For our departure EvD had rented a typical American 'supercruiser'. But this car had some dirty tricks in store for us. All of the controls and appointments were automatic, even the seat belts.

Von Däniken sat at the wheel ready to go, but his two companions, Ernsting and I, were still battling with the safety belts. It was necessary to first buckle the damned thing and then let it find its correct position. Easier said than done. You pulled the belt out, tried to hook it—zick, zack, it slipped through clumsy fingers and was all coiled up again in its retainer. Try again. Same lack of success. And of course the engine could not be started until the belts were fastened.

Finally Ernsting attempted to outwit the 'Detroit monster'. He carefully withdrew the belt and hooked it together behind him. The motor still refused to start. Gnashing his teeth, he commenced the original procedure over again. Flip-flop, zick-zack—and the super-cruiser remained glued to the spot. We could see our probably ludicrous expressions reflected in the face of our chauffeur. Däniken sat there and laughed till the tears came.

Eventually we got under way. Ernsting tried again to mislead our vehicle by stealthily loosening his seat-belt during the ride, but of course the motor struck once more. You can't fool a computer.

When EvD is on the road, no matter whether he's tracking his gods or on a lecture tour, he always tries to give as good as he gets. Eduardo Chaves, an amiable young Portuguese living in Rio de Janeiro, dates his acquaintanceship with von Däniken by a blue-black bruise on his shoulder. Chaves had waited in the air terminal for the Swiss to arrive, and greeted him effusively. Däniken responded with the same enthusiasm, rather painfully for the Brazilian. 'Although I felt that friendly shoulder-pat for two days afterward, I didn't let it distress me—perhaps such greetings were a Swiss or Germanic folk-custom.' Chaves tried to make me (and himself) believe.

Although Däniken spent eight days in Rio, he was able to spare only a scant half-day for his Portuguese friend. Here, as he does everywhere, EvD took pains to learn the customs and idiosyncrasies of the Brazilians. As an admirer of the soccer artistry of the famous Pele, he of course obtained tickets to the Rio Stadium, where with 180,000 other enthusiasts he roared at the players vying for the leather sphere.

Däniken spent a full week in Piauhi, a province in the northeast of the country. Located there is Brazil's best-known and best preserved archaeological zone, Sete Cidades National Park. And of course visits to various museums were also on the Swiss traveller's agenda.

Von Däniken had trouble only with waiters. An observation of his friend Chaves, with which I concur: 'I have the feeling that Erich is always tempted to check the knowledge and efficiency of his former colleagues.' Chaves attributes these Däniken-tests to his former success in the gastronomic field. This is quite possible. In any case, EvD was highly vexed when a waiter at Rio's Sheraton Hotel brought no cream for his coffee, although cream had been specifically requested. When he complained, he was told that there was no cream in the house.

Of course the former hotel manager knew that coffee is customarily served black in Brazil—but he insisted that his order be filled. Yes *sir*, but you must wait a short while.

Although his coffee was almost cold, the cream finally arrived. It was beamingly served to him, beamingly Däniken poured it into his cup, sipped, and grimaced painfully—the cream was sour.

This episode did not discourage him, however, from spending his few unscheduled hours visiting night-clubs, good restaurants and even snack-bars. Only one pleasure-spot he couldn't find—a casino. Gambling is officially not permitted in Brazil.

Yugoslavia is another story. EvD's secretary Dünnenberger tells of a memorable evening there with his boss.

'After our exhausting Kashmir trip we drove home to Switzerland, and our road led through Tito-land. Dog-tired, we arrived one evening at Zagreb's Intercontinental Hotel. A long dusty day lay behind us. With our last reserves of energy we dragged ourselves to the dinner table. Suddenly Erich was wide awake. He'd read a little notice on a card beside the menu that the hotel boasted a gaming room on its seventeenth floor. Erich's spirits soared again. No one should get the impression, however, that Däniken is a reckless, hare-brained gambler. At the roulette table he has a daring but analytical style of play.

'We changed floors and exchanged a hundred dollars. Däniken said with assurance, "We'll quickly lose these hundred piastres, and then to bed." ' Said, but not done. EvD sat himself at the table, ordered a bottle of red wine, and at first limited his action to just watching the course of the little white ball. A quarter of an hour later he placed his first bet. Meanwhile, Willi Dünnenberger yawned heart-rendingly, longing for his soft bed.

A half-hour later the weary warrior had forgotten his longing, and his attention was riveted on the fateful ball. It spun, and dropped, and the counters piled up in front of his chief. The Goddess of Fortune was with Däniken on that evening. The well-known quotation was confirmed once more: 'To him that hath shall be given.'

EvD sat . . . and won. He continued to sit . . . and won as much again. It just couldn't last. Dünnenberger watched as the stacks of *jetons* towered before EvD.

The salon had almost emptied. Around this single roulette table were two other guests besides Däniken, His secretary remained a silent though observant bystander. Not Willi alone—all the Casino personnel had noted the run of luck of the short stout gentleman at the table, and had gathered around the three players. The word was soon passed about, 'That's *Däniken* who's winning so much!' EvD tried to lose. He risked large stakes from his winnings, and mimed to Dünnenberger, 'There must be some way of losing the damned money!'

There didn't seem to be. Forty-five minutes later there were 223,000 dinars-worth of counters stacked in front of Däniken, about 30,000 marks. And then he dropped the bombshell. He stood up abruptly, looked about into the awed and attentive faces of the casino employees —and made a speech. Explosive and in this country, heretical. Karl Marx would not have been overjoyed. Or perhaps he would.

'This capital here,' he began, 'I haven't really earned. It increased without my producing anything of value. But I'm a believer in the principle of useful production. Whoever works and produces shall be paid for his efforts accordingly. But whoever gains money without working for it is an exploiter, a profiteer.

'Look around at yourselves. The genuine exploiters stand on the Left; they are Marxists. Marxists who do nothing productive, just redistribute both real and non-existent capital. Believe me, there is no greater exploiter-nation than one which depicts itself as super-socialistic. Be truthful—is there a single worker here in the East who leads a better life than his counterpart in the West? Is this the way a "Workers' Paradise" is supposed to operate?'

The casino employees stood as if struck by lightning. No one had ever served them up so much 'class-enemy' politics at one time. But then came the evening's climax: before any of his audience had time to think of a retort, von Däniken, smiling, pressed 30,000 dinars in each one's hand. Of course, he couldn't forgo accompanying his 'donation' with the words: 'Here, take the money! It was unfairly earned, without my working for it!'

At this moment the Swiss had completely forgotten that elsewhere, a few short weeks ago, he had missed by a hair being plundered of all his possessions. This happened after the journey to Kashmir's temple of Ezekiel. They were on the stretch from Lahore to Quetta, and in order to cross the flooded Chenab River it had been necessary to make a 250-kilometre detour via the bridge at Alipur. All the Indus River bridges but one had been washed away or were under water, and after many hours of further detours to reach that crossing, they finally arrived at the provincial town of Dera Ghazi Khan. It was a cheerless-looking settlement. Along the road around little campfires, pitiful vendors offered fruit and produce for sale. Dully and hostilely they stared at the travellers. A youngster hesitantly informed them with a few words of broken English, that there was a first-class hotel, the Shezan.

It was first class all right—infected with first-class bugs and lice and supremely filthy. In the central court there was a dry and crumbling fountain. EvD insisted that he be allowed to park the car inside the courtyard, and that the iron gate at the entrance be closed. A compassionate Pakistani who spoke fluent English told them that it was well to take such precautions, as many travellers had already been robbed here, and the authorities seemed to be powerless against these criminal activities.

'Those were indeed happy tidings,' said Dünnenberger. For the first time on the trip Däniken put the loaded gas-pistol under his pillow. Both of them slept fitfully that night. And both of them woke at the same time—something was happening in the courtyard. A look through the window banished their weariness. Muffled figures scurried through the court, clustered around the car. Däniken grabbed the weapon. 'He slipped the pistol under his shirt and went outside; I followed at his heels. Suddenly, a rattling as of chains, a shout, the court brightly lit by a carbide lamp, dazzling as a floodlight. Four swaddled forms stood around the Range Rover. A threatening situation. We took our courage in both hands. Erich showed his pistol, I held a spray-can of tear gas at the ready. The mummies held a violent discussion. Fear of our weapons turned the tide, and the whole gang retreated.'

As Däniken suspected that they'd gone for reinforcements, they threw their things together and departed immediately.

I have before me a picture postcard of the ruins at Persepolis. EvD and Willi sent it to me shortly after their Srinagar adventure. Written across the back are words that hit the mark: 'May we not have before us what is behind us!'

I mentioned earlier that Däniken the epicure and former hotelier could always find fault with his former colleagues wherever he went. What Chaves had observed in Rio and what I could corroborate from our American tour, secretary Dünnenberger describes in his own graphic style.

'The hardships of the journey took their toll. We had flown on a brief side-trip to Calcutta and Delhi for scheduled lectures and when we returned to Srinagar, Erich fell ill. I rushed him back to our room in the Oberoi Hotel. His head looked like a ripe tomato: the fever thermometer read 39.8° (103.6° Fahrenheit). He swallowed an assortment of antibiotics from our portable drugstore and went to bed with icebags on his feet and forehead. This reduced the fever temporarily, but it soon regained its former high level. It was August 16, 1975, and the next day he had an appointment with Professor F. H. Hassnain, a Pakistani archaeologist at the University of Srinagar. Erich phoned, explained his condition and begged to be excused.

'Two hours later Dr Miray-u-din, Director of the Srinagar Clinic, arrived at his bedside. The good doctor informed us that neither European nor American medicines had any effect against Indian viruses, and prescribed some local nostrums. Shortly thereafter the nightstand held eight tubes and bottles, whose contents Erich swallowed.'

Now EvD became grouchy over his helpless state, and even more so because of the Hotel Oberoi's service and personnel. If a bowl of ice was ordered, two dishes of rice were served; a request for iced tea brought a bellboy with lotus blossoms in a vase. When Däniken asked for some fruit salad, they fetched a local newspaper, illegible to him. He called for the reception clerk and told him in person what he wanted. 'Okay, sir!' A half-hour later a page ushered a taxidriver into the sickroom, who insisted that he had been called for. That slip-up cost ten rupees.

Although Däniken's fever gradually subsided, he still felt miserable. He felt neither hunger nor thirst, and wanted only to sleep. Sleep—no way! Sometimes there were as many as six room orderlies around the bed, one dusting the fan-blades, another tucking in the sheet, a third moving flowers from one table to another. All of them stared at him, and hung around waiting for *baksheesh*.

Luckily Professor Hassnain paid a visit during this chaos. With a few emphatic words he got rid of the whole crew. 'One has to know Urdu,' sighed Willi in doleful remembrance.

Erich's knees shake even today, thinking back to that lecture evening in Calcutta when he spoke before a throng of several thousand fanatical devotees. 'I believe that situation was more dangerous for Erich and me than the one in Dera Ghazi Khan defending our Range Rover,' thinks Däniken's travelling companion. He's right beyond doubt, for wedged tightly in that mass of humans, weapons would have been useless.

At noon an EvD reception committee had shown up at his hotel—two archaeologists, two anthropologists, a museum director and several assistants. They assured him that all the preparations had been made for his lecture.

Willi Dünnenberger: 'Erich would have so liked to explore Calcutta, India's largest city, but it was simply impossible. He wasn't able to step out of the hotel room; journalists kept a tight grip on the door handle, radio reporters held microphones to his lips.' What he said in that day's interviews made the front pages the next day. Of course he only knew this from the accompanying photos, as the text was in Bengali. Although the world traveller speaks five languages, the Bengali script was beyond him. What was said about him? English-speaking reporters assured him that all the comment was favourable.

EvD was curious as to what 'preparations had been made'. His expectations dissolved in panic at six that evening as he, secretary Willi and the reception committee drove up to the museum where his lecture was to be given. Indira Gandhi would have burst with envy. It was like a diplomatic reception. Only with much more turmoil.

'Even before our car came to a halt, it was wedged in among thousands of people,' related Dünnenberger. 'The police had their hands full—they conveyed us into a central courtyard and cordoned off the mob behind two long lines, between which we were squeezed into the auditorium. Believe you me, I've never before been through anything like it, and neither has Erich. The spacious lecture hall was almost indescribable, its steps, galleries, even window ledges lined to overflowing with human beings. The air was oppressive; hot, humid and motionless, and thick enough to cut. But where was Erich?'

The seething crowd had separated the secretary from his chief. Dünnenberger was wearing a bright red pullover as visible as a stoplight, so that EvD could pick him out in the crowd. While he scuffled with enthusiastic students for a place to stand, Däniken was being towed to the front of the hall. There, before an enormous screen, stood four chairs; EvD was unceremoniously pressed into one.

'Before Erich could speak he had to listen to laudatory introductions given by an anthropologist (a woman), an archaeologist and the museum director,' recounted his secretary. 'They all extolled him in a manner downright embarrassing. He wasn't able to say a word for several minutes—the ovation was so thunderous that the microphone would not have amplified his voice enough for him to be heard.' It

35

was clear to Däniken that under these conditions he'd better give only a short version of his slide-lecture, which he did. At the end a wild tumult, broke out. Thousands crushed toward him.

Dünnenberger: 'I waved my arms, even used my fists, trying to reach the podium. No chance. Hours later in our hotel room, Erich told me of his emotions during those minutes. Until that moment he hadn't known how much one could fear one's fellow man. I felt and feel the same way. Whoever has not experienced such a thing himself cannot possibly imagine it.'

The weight of the crowd had borne Däniken to the floor. He crouched on all fours, bathed in sweat, in imminent danger of being squashed flat by his fans. He crawled into a corner, where the precarious protection of two walls granted him a temporary breathing spell.

The police had not been standing idly by. Truncheons swung through the air, drumming a staccato ruffle on the backs of the unruly mob. They remained unmoved, intent on their target: Erich von Däniken. It was a shocking and frightful scene. The police finally hacked an aisle through the crowd, and Willi and EvD were able to escape to their car, where they sat soaked in sweat while it brought them back to the hotel by the speediest route. Their clothes, including Willi's red sweater hung in tatters.

All during the next day, the two thought apprehensively of that evening's lecture, to be given at the University of Calcutta. Groundlessly, as it turned out. When they were unable to alight from their student-besieged car, the police again made way for them—in a manner unfriendly, to say the least. The students were not in the least discouraged. They shouted in unison: 'Long live Däniken!'

The god-seeker spoke for two hours, and the capacious hall, filled to overflowing, was still as still could be. This was the Nuclear Physics auditorium, the largest hall in the University, and the University itself is the largest and oldest in Asia, with two hundred and forty thousand students.

'Don't ask how it went after the lecture,' said EvD's good right hand Dünnenberger. 'The enthusiasm was indescribable. Erich signed autographs until his fingers grew numb.'

Däniken: 'Later, among the faculty heads, I was lapped with a wave of sympathetic and co-operative feeling. Professors were ready and eager to aid me with their specific branches of knowledge. Researchers in Sanskrit offered to supply me with an abundance of material from all over India. And the Dean asserted that the theories in my books were to Hindus *realities*, whose wider dissemination he had long awaited.'

To this day EvD maintains an extensive correspondence with many of these Indian and Pakistani scholars and scientists. Professor Hassnain, mentioned earlier, has recently written that starting with Däniken's initial encouragement, he has been raising funds to dispatch a crane and heavy-equipment crew to raise the giant monolith at Srinagar's 'Hebrew' temple, and perhaps unlock the mystery of the radioactive traces.

Travels with Däniken offer something for everyone. And, thank the Lord, they are not always frightening and perilous. Hans Neuner, who accompanied EvD on his first searches for traces of the gods, told me of one delightful episode, although the circumstances which led to it were certainly far from pleasant.

'It was 1967. Erich and I were under way on the *Carretera Central*, a Peruvian railroad which was at that time absolutely unenjoyable. We were riding from 11,000-foot Cuzco, the old capital of the Inca Empire, up to Puno on Lake Titicaca. The coaches stank horribly, and we were both happy to finally arrive at our destination, the boat terminal where we would embark for the lake crossing to Bolivia. Erich had booked a first-class cabin, which proved to be a dark narrow dungeon with four plank bunks in two tiers, one pair already occupied by local Indians. Not only by Indians, as we soon learned, but also by an assortment of vermin. As sleeping there was out of the question, we went above and lay down dog-tired on the also filthy open deck.

Then suddenly we heard a woman weeping, and a man's voice attempting to comfort her in authentic Basel dialect. Now, you know, if a Swiss meets a countryman in distress, even at the other end of the world—at least a Swiss such as Erich—he offers a helping hand. What he learned from the two touched his heart; the young couple were on their honeymoon. What the husband had thought would be exotic enchantment—a honeymoon night on romantic Lake Titicaca—had proved to be a nightmare. The young groom had booked second-class passage, probably for reasons of economy. They were shocked to discover that they were compelled to do what Erich and I were doing involuntarily—sleep on deck. There were no cabins for second-class passengers.

Erich knew exactly what to do. He climbed down to our cell, induced the Indian occupants to vacate their bunks with a bottle of

Pisco, the local *schnapps*, and offered our lodgings to his loving compatriots. They said it was the greatest and most generous wedding gift they could ever imagine.

Early next morning the luxury liner docked in Gaqui harbour on the Bolivian side. We saw the couple for the last time. They waved goodbye, the bride a little pale, her husband with an embarrassed smile. We supposed that they hadn't had much sleep.

Exactly nine months later our suppositions were confirmed. A birth announcement arrived from Basel. Erich showed me the sweet 'souvenir', which had been sent by the Swiss couple. It showed a baby sitting upon a little pot, with the caption 'Product of Lake Titicaca'. The proud parents had christened their little daughter 'Titi'.

It should never be said that Däniken has done nothing for Swiss posterity. He has—although in a roundabout way.

CHAPTER III

Däniken—Sometimes a Private Person

To know Erich von Däniken better, to occasionally spend time in his company, requires an ability to make instantaneous changes of pace. That statement should be taken literally; the successful Swiss author measures the tempo of his life according to other standards. 'The end justifies the means'—that saying, used in its benign sense, could have been invented expressly for Däniken. He lives and acts in a state of urgency.

'I am one possessed, I want to know everything—and as I grow older, the more greedy for knowledge I become. I have the fear that Time is running away from me, and I will remain behind in a void, not having used Time to the fullest. . . .' Erich von Däniken did *not* say that; the words are those of the creator of the world-famous *West Side Story*, Leonard Bernstein. Although the gifted composer and director is not even acquainted with Däniken, parallels between the two personalities cannot be denied. What Bernstein said could have been said by Däniken, word for word. For it is in accord with the tenor of his life.

'I am torn apart—I want to do so much. But one cannot escape the shackles with which one is bound.' Another *cri de coeur* of the driven Bernstein that might have come from the lips of the Swiss globetrotter. For Erich von Däniken is also torn in many directions—and yet for past (and surely for future) years has been shackled by the bonds of a 'God-investigator', compelled to follow the one-way street of his calling.

'It's exhausting to be famous. It requires effort which one could put to better use.' Or: 'I live under constant tension, and fear that one day it will snap. . . .' Two more sentiments of Leonard Bernstein. But they are shocking for someone like me, who places himself within the close circle around the most successful post-war, non-fiction author. About thirty-seven million copies of books produced in Däniken's 'God-workshop'—he's written six so far—have been published all over the world. In the United States alone almost thirteen million. Today the God-seeker is a millionaire several times over, although he doesnt live like one. His house in the small suburban village of Bonstetten, a'half-hour's train ride from Zürich, is surrounded by far more extravagant family dwellings. Däniken's two-story domicile lacks any suggestion of ostentation or obtrusiveness; everything is subordinate to comfort.

As a rule one imagines a millionaire's villa otherwise. Can a house erected on a 1700-square-foot lot—one twenty-fifth of an acre—properly even be described as a 'villa'? This question occurs to the visitor, as he stands for the first time before the garden gate of the Däniken residence in Bonstetten's Stallikonerstrasse. A wide driveway lies in front of him, wide because place must be found for two 'petrol-coaches'. Last year this space was occupied by a bulky Range Rover.

To enter the house one must first mount eleven steps. The entrance hall is small, most of it taken up by a brightly-covered mattress for the weightiest item on Däniken's animate inventory—the Great Dane Neptun. Adjoining is a cloakroom, in constant use; prominent persons from lands all over the world have hung their coats here.

To the right, the kitchen. Not large, but equipped with the latest in appliances and labour-saving devices. Customarily a woman's domain, but not here. Wife Elisabeth, dubbed 'Ebet' by the master of the house, gladly shares the kitchen realm with her spouse during his infrequent stopovers at home. Without doing his wife an injustice, Erich von Däniken truly enjoys his own artistry as a cook. When the two of them together get busy on the kitchen-range—as happened on June 1st, 1975, when they were obliged to feed a group of at least thirty visitors —the memory alone inspires in me a feeling of hunger.

So let us quickly leave the kitchen and enter the all-purpose living room. No door separates it from the entrance hall; an open archway bares to view all the hospitable furnishings this visiting-room contains. Conspicuous is the huge fireplace whose appearance—white with roughcast mortar hood, the mantel an oaken tie 'liberated' from some abandoned railway line—reveals the interior-decorating talent of Ebet, who surprised her Erich with this novel effect upon his return from an American lecture-tour.

To the right of the fireplace, in a corner which a great window dominates, a modern dining-table with six comfortable chairs. Everything in white. On the left of the fireplace the room broadens out, and is taken up by a conversation-corner—two sofas and a long table with four armchairs. One feels at ease in all this spaciousness.

The walls are lined with shelves. They hold—as one would expect in an author's home—his own works. The wall is four metres long and two high, and its shelves are reserved for editions of Däniken's books which have been published in languages other than German. The greater part of them Däniken cannot read. To date twenty-six (!) translations exist.

The host leads his visitor through the entire house. The floor above is reached by way of a circular staircase. To conserve space it describes but a half-circle. In front is the room of Cornelia, 14-year-old pride of the family. The world of Lela (nickname of the sports-mad teenager) shows itself to be a light, friendly, happy one, her room papered in optimistic colours and appointed with unmistakable signs of youth— pop-art posters on the walls, costumed dolls and a menagerie of stuffed animals. A Salzburg-doll was my contribution.

Distances Papa Däniken traverses best by auto, his daughter covers effortlessly on foot. In 1975 the indolent EvD nearly burst with pride; Lela won the 80-metre finals for 11-to-15-year-olds, and was crowned Swiss champion. Her father has similar ambitions only in the presence of photo-journalists. Then he plays at gymnastics, and hints that amateur athletics is his secret passion. . . .

Next to Lela's room, her parents' bedroom. A man often slinks on tiptoe into this room, usually about four in the morning, and slithers quietly between the sheets of the marriage-bed. Another work-'day' has ended for Erich von Däniken.

Slyly the man of the house pilots us one floor higher—into the attic. It has attained new prestige in Däniken's home. Months prior to Christmas 1975 EvD was surprised by an unusual request from his wife: Would you give me 5000 francs? I need it for your Christmas present.

Although he wondered, the one appealed to as usual couldn't say no. 5000 'piastres' (as EvD calls all the world's currencies) changed hands.

The months went by. Erich von Däniken was away on a long round of talks and appearances. He arrived home again just two days before Christmas Eve. The Yule celebration passed harmoniously; but for *what* had he paid 5000 francs? Wife Ebet gestured for silence and said 'Come with me'.

She led Erich up to the attic. It no longer looked as it had. Däniken suddenly found himself in an artist's studio. All the necessary materials were at hand. 'Transforming an attic into a studio costs money,' explained his wife, 'but it was worth it.'

EvD is filled with admiration for Ebet's clever plan to tie him more securely to home with the aid of brush and pigment. The first stirrings of artistic ambitions are already perceptible. Däniken thinks fleetingly of the works of art which will one day adorn his God-workshop. Who knows, perhaps in a few years the *cognoscenti* will consider it prestigious to be able to hang 'a Däniken'. As a picture, of course.

The god-researcher's real centre of activity is in the cellar. There he puts down on paper what he has investigated and collated. These 'cosmic depths' are also reached via a circular stairway. A thick carpet muffles annoying sounds. Please do not disturb—in Däniken's cellar-study concentrated work is done; we are in an inner sanctum. Utz Utermann, who inclines toward statistics, was here with his tape measure. The office space is 10.5 metres long, 5.5 metres wide, 1.85 metres (a fraction over six feet) high. There is no danger that the room's principal user will bump his head against the ceiling. Even the 'top deck' of EvD-computer Dünnenberger is a few safe centimetres short.

Willi Dünnenberger is readily labelled a first-prizewinner by his travel-happy chief. He combines all the qualities Däniken silently hoped for when he first advertised for an efficient secretary.

Before me lies the newspaper advertisement which determined the future course of Dünnenberger's life. It reads:

> You can be as young or as old as you feel, and of the sex with which you were born. You shall maintain my German and English correspondence (predominantly by dictation), catalogue and arrange my new records, and gradually become my indispensable right hand. You will work only in your boss's office, and he, a controversial author, is travelling much of the time.
>
> Especially valued in you are patience, reasoning ability and honesty.
>
> We work a thirty-seven hour week. Payment according to current standards and three weeks vacation the first year are points of honour. Start work as soon as engaged. Typewritten applications are more acceptable to me than illegible handwriting. Include photograph, and send to:
> Erich von Däniken, 8906 Bonstetten. . . .

The archives of the Swiss god-seeker are nothing of which he need be ashamed. Whoever seeks anything there is sure to find it, if the item sought is listed in the catalogue. Astro-archaeologists find in Däniken's cellar well-ordered files in their sphere of interest. Each of the archive cabinets is twenty drawers high and six wide. Willi has done his duty admirably as archivist. Each drawer is clearly identified with colour-coded letters and numbers, everything in fool-proof order.

Before digging through the files, one refers to a catalogue which holds archive-cards—like road-maps in a way—listed according to about 10,000 key-words. Thanks to Dünnenberger's easily-read hiero-glyphics, theme-classification, authors' names and other data are effortlessly located. 'I've had lifelong involvement with archives of all kinds,' states Utermann, 'and I can say that I've never known a better-arranged or more practicable one.' He is thoroughly enthusiastic about Däniken's 'household pharmacy', as he disrespectfully calls the archives.

His compliment is aimed at the head of the house as well as at his closest co-worker. Accuracy is the first priority in this office. Willi Dünnenberger's sense of order is treasured by his boss, whose advertise-ment could hardly have brought a better response.

There is also a file for all sorts of photographs in the archives. A place is provided for seven special still cameras, and 8 mm and 16 mm motion-picture cameras. They are indispensable to Däniken, and the numerous illustrations in EvD's books show what they have been able to accomplish. Erich von Däniken has become a competent and respected photo-journalist.

To the average person, EvD's time schedule is upside down. At a time when other people are switching off their TVs before hopping into bed, Däniken is just becoming really alert. He sits down at his desk in a chair whose base rests on casters, and dictates new ideas into his mini-recorder. He sips now and then from a glass of red wine (from his own temperature-controlled cellar) and draws at his unique pipe, whose bowl bears an amazing resemblance to an American space capsule. Only at the first hint of dawn does Däniken think of going to bed.

'May heaven preserve you from the eventuality that an extra-terrestrial decides to land at your door in the morning. You would sleep right through the divine visitation.' I couldn't resist teasing him. It was no use, of course. EvD is almost never roused from his bed before 11 am. I can still hear his lament when in the USA he was startled out of a sound sleep at seven in the morning so that he could take part in a TV talk-show.

His wife Ebet accepts EvD the way he is. 'If he would only really enjoy staying home,' she sighs, with good reason. At half-past ten on New Year's Eve, 1974, Elisabeth von Däniken produced this statistic. 'This is our 116th supper together,' she told her spouse. 116 evenings at home out of 365. Von Däniken has promised many times to do better, and he is sincere in his good intentions. However, when EvD does remain at home for several days, perhaps even for weeks, then he wants to know nothing of the clamour and turmoil of the world outside. He encapsulates himself, and it is often a great effort for his wife to move him even to visit friends. She isn't cross because of it— 'After all, he is so seldom at home,' she says understandingly.

It is not so remarkable that another utterance of Bernstein's fits Däniken in another context. For he is also a 'jet-set traveller', a 'VIP'.

Jet-setting is exciting. One encounters so many people around the globe. But it is also depressing. Thereby the frantic, unremitting time-machine is set in motion. One no longer lives, one is *lived*. Only occasionally one succeeds in escaping from the orbit. Then I'm with my family again. . . .

In 1969, after my first exchange of correspondence with Däniken, I was also subjected to a 'change of pace'. Since his spectacular arrest months earlier at Vienna's Schwechat Airport, I had taken a lively interest in the affair. At that time I was the editor of a Viennese daily (now no longer in existence). To me EvD was a blank page. I had had no contact whatsoever with him—except that I had read his first book. I was not so much interested in Däniken's proof of innocence as I was puzzled (as were my colleagues) over the actual motives behind his internment.

—Were there religious, commercial or personal enmities involved?
—Why do the Swiss authorities persist in remaining silent?
—Had it really been necessary, because of 6000 francs in overdue resort taxes, to set Interpol on the track of the Davos hotel lessee?

Remanded into investigative custody in Vienna, Erich von Däniken asserted his innocence. He demanded that he be extradited to Swiss jurisdiction, and he also protested at the denial of this demand, in those hand-written letters which he forwarded to me from his cell in the provincial courthouse. Shortly before, I had sent him a copy of the newspaper containing an article I had written, whose headline asked the question: 'Campaign Against Best-selling Author?'

'My present situation is catastrophic for me,' wrote Däniken, and 'I can honestly assure you that rank injustice is being done me by the

Davos Examining Magistrate's office ... when I first heard of this denunciation, I honestly believed that it was a jest. It simply could not be! I had continued to keep to the payment schedule agreed upon with the Resort Association. Why, it follows that complaints would have to be filed against a quarter of the Davos hoteliers!'

To quote here all the sordid details of the administrative methods of Swiss justice, with Däniken's deadly enemy Kirchhofer at the helm, oversteps the bounds I've set myself. (Erich von Däniken will do this at the end of the book: 'It was really like this'.)

At any rate, my written contact with the Swiss god-seeker was broken off for the time being. Däniken was extradited to Switzerland, and a year later there was a sensational trial which, because of the way it was run, I saw fit to describe in print as a 'witch-trial'. Erich von Däniken was sentenced to three and a half years in prison, and subsequently transferred to Regensdorf Penitentiary near Zürich. There my second letter reached the prominent prisoner.

For years—independent of Däniken's interest in the subject—I had occupied myself with the theme of Astronaut-Gods. A first treatise, initially an interpretation of Ezekiel's reports in the Old Testament, had been published in a 1967 science-fiction magazine. I had sent this article together with my newspaper report to Däniken, during his Vienna imprisonment in January 1969. Meanwhile the brief Ezekiel article had grown into a 180-page manuscript. Besides the tale of the Biblical prophet, it included attempts to interpret or explain other Old Testament episodes, and it even gave a sketchy Jesus-hypothesis. The small volume, called *Gott kam von den Sternen* (*God Came From the Stars*), was published later that year, and on September 17, 1970, I sent it together with another letter to Regensdorf. Scarcely a week later I held Däniken's answer, dated September 20, in my hands. In it, the god-seeker granted me his express permission to utilise his train of thought at my discretion, to put it to good use if needed.

... Be reassured that I have no thoughts of 'competition' or anything remotely similar; to me that is utter nonsense. You can help yourself to anything of mine that you need or desire, whether it's from my books, written or yet-to-be-written, or from our future conversations. For ME [at times EvD uses capitals for emphasis] there is no such thing as intimations of plagiarism. That is childishness, and has no place among adults turned in the same direction. You can therefore put THESE worries confidently out of your mind. And should anyone ever whisper, 'He got that from Däniken', just laugh in his face and answer, 'Däniken is my friend!'

I frankly admit that I had not sent my Swiss pen-pal *Gott kam von den Sternen* altogether selflessly. What I sent was expanded to book-length and published five years later by Hermann Bauer under the same title. I hoped to beguile von Däniken into writing a Foreword to this anticipated future edition, so I had concocted a little stratagem. My letter said, namely, that I wasn't too satisfied with the Foreword contained in my minor opus; I hoped for the same reaction from Regensdorf. My wish bore fruit. EvD responded in the vehement fashion to be expected from him in his second letter of November 2, 1970. He had read my work, and commented:

... Basically, my compliments. You have offered here several splendid subjects. ...

Then came what I wanted to read:

... but I find completely superfluous and distasteful your entire 'preparatory' explanation. Rank apologies for what you're presenting —where no apologies are necessary! Explanations that you do NOT wish to offend—explanations which strike just those you're trying to appease! ...

My seedling had fallen on fertile ground; now I had only to wait until it sprouted.

What I liked then about Erich von Däniken was his disarming honesty. No flowery phrases such as, 'In your place I would have formulated the Foreword somewhat differently, and so on, and so on ...' Instead, a few hardly-flattering words, by which I felt in no way injured. On the contrary—I was impressed by this openness, these unvarnished statements. Däniken simply wrote his opinion. He glossed over nothing. He praised what he liked and criticised what he disagreed with.

The Swiss has remained so to this very day: straightforward and blunt. This is probably the chief reason why no one is merely lukewarm towards him and his theories. He has only unconditional admirers and implacable opponents.

The seedling sprouted. Däniken's third letter reached me on February 11, 1971. By then the 180 pages of my self-published mini-book had grown to over 300. The manuscript was with Herbig

Publishers in Munich. I had reported this to EvD, then sat back and hoped. He wrote:

> . . . you report that perhaps Herbig will accept your manuscript. . . . Now I ask myself whether it would be helpful to you, Mr Krassa, where I to write a Foreword to your book. . . .

Things didn't go well at Herbig, however, and it took another three-and-a-half years before *Gott kam von den Sternen* was actually in the bookshops. But Däniken kept his pledge; he wrote the promised Foreword.

CHAPTER IV

Friendship is not an Empty Word

He himself denies it firmly and repeatedly; the huge amount of wealth ascribed to him is a myth. But he does have enough money to be able to live his life as he wishes. Erich von Däniken practises unpretentiousness. He knows what he wants.

Certainly his 37 million internationally-published books have made him a millionaire (in Swiss francs). And he wouldn't be a practical Swiss if he had not known how to invest his 'piastres' profitably—stocks, land, deposits—as would anyone in a similar position.

Whoever has money doesn't lack for vicious gossip, it springs up of itself. One hears about Däniken that he's avaricious, that all his efforts are designed solely to increase his bank balance. Ideals are foreign to him. His Astronaut-Gods are a fake. He writes only because of money. The envy-complex blooms, and the plant is nursed and nurtured by ill wishers. To all such detractors I say: being wealthy is an obligation to no one. Even if EvD were actually a Swiss 'Scotsman' (forgive the use of the proverbial expression!), that would still be his own affair.

However, von Däniken acts out of character as a rich man. He has enough money to live on, and somewhat more in bank deposits—but generosity is not a quality he holds lightly. He gladly helps whomever and wherever he can, and this help is not limited just to friends and associates. He offers help spontaneously; spontaneity is part of his nature.

In 1968 he read in *Sputnik*, the Soviet counterpart to *Reader's Digest*, a report about the discovery of mysterious stone plates in the Chinese–Tibetan border area Bayan-Khara-Ula. The report mentioned that Russian ancient-historian Alexander Kasanzhev knew something about the find. Däniken grabbed the telephone, booked a seat on an upcoming flight, and a few days later was Kasanzhev's guest in Moscow.

Though EvD is occupied by weighty matters, he doesn't ignore people or things of lesser import. Once he was driving with Willi through Zürich, and saw an old, poorly-clad woman rummaging in a dustbin. She was searching for salvageable articles discarded by more prosperous folk. Däniken reacted instantly, slamming on his brakes and jumping from the car. 'Here, granny,' he said precipitately, pressing a 100-franc note into the bewildered woman's hand, 'take this and buy yourself a few nice things.' He was back in the car and away before she could thank him.

'That's simply the way he is,' says his secretary Dünnenberger. He values his chief's generosity without overlooking its drawbacks. 'Unfortunately—or perhaps fortunately—it's one of his minor weaknesses; he can't handle money very well. In a nutshell: he's not the frugal type.'

Däniken's liberality, on which he places no restrictions, can also prove to be a boomerang. Utz Utermann put it succinctly: 'Anyone who takes the trouble can draw Erich out like a Christmas goose. Sad to say, this has happened more than once.' So if one looks for 'flaws' in the Swiss author, here they are: generosity and an excess of good nature. The two are not always compatible. Utermann: 'But perhaps these "Achilles-heels" belong to his being, his character. Were Erich otherwise, he would not be the person he is.'

Among those who have learned better to know and value EvD is of course his publisher, Erwin Barth von Wehrenalp. The ECON-boss even sees positive points in Däniken's weaknesses.

'I hold EvD to be a man who knows what every Swiss knows well— the value of a franc. On the other hand, I have seldom met anyone who is as generous in money matters. Toward his family, naturally; but Däniken does even more for friends than they expect of him.'

And Eduardo Chaves sends this fan-letter from Rio: 'In my opinion, Erich is a master of life. He knows how to accept and enjoy this life the way it is—and lets others live theirs.'

It may be that many who classify EvD as extravagant also depict him as thoughtless and frivolous. Whoever does so, is someone who does not know him, someone who hasn't fathomed the Swiss's lifestyle. 'Money's meaning doesn't lie in hoarding it,' says EvD, 'but simply and solely in the ability to spend it for suitable purposes.' Despite all the contingency reserves the god-seeker has invested—'There must always be enough to live comfortably and well for one year,' is his maxim—his wallet serves chiefly as a temporary resting place for its contents. Däniken's investigative work, however one may regard it, costs something. But the author with royalties counted in millions can state with pride that he has viewed personally every place on earth where traces of his Astronaut-Gods supposedly exist. For this he can give thanks to his personal view of the uses of money.

He hasn't forgotten his family for one moment in this regard. In case one day something should befall him—which because of his extensive travelling is an ever-present possibility—his wife and daughter will certainly not go hungry. For he has drawn up an unusual agreement: While he lives, all income from the sale of hardbound Däniken books in America (the greater income is, of course, derived from paperbacks) is automatically deposited in his wife's bank account. This account is at her sole disposal, and is no concern of her husband's.

Walter Ernsting: 'His generosity has more than once been put to the test—not only by me but by others, even strangers. It seems that Däniken, having attained a comparatively prosperous position due to the success of his books, selflessly lets others have a share in it. He is not miserly, and in my personal experience Erich has proved to be a good, true and reliable friend.'

His impulse to offer help wherever he sees the need for it has often landed Däniken in serious trouble. He helps unconditionally, friends or strangers, it doesn't matter which. The following really belongs in a chapter on his travels, but I feel that the episode characterises very well Däniken's attitude towards his fellow-man. Far from incurious, he sympathises *and* empathises with the problems of others. This is not to say he intrudes—as many do nowadays—but rather tenders whatever assistance he can to whoever is in need.

It was during Däniken's fatiguing journey through Pakistan; under way to Quetta, with numerous involuntary detours. A German couple named Bultmann were also trying for the same destination. The young pair had apparently confused the trip over the blazing, flooded terrain with a weekend outing. Just as EvD had not spared funds, time or preparation in order to make the expedition as endurable as possible for him and his associate, just so 'unencumbered' had the German tourists embarked on their pleasure-jaunt. In a white Mercedes-Benz, and with a black terrier as mascot.

The Bultmanns' airy attitude was disconcerting, but Däniken made the best of it, and invited them to follow behind the Range Rover, which they did. At first everything went smoothly—as smoothly as could be expected on a highway lacking all roadside amenities.

The two-unit convoy rolled toward Sukkur along the Indus River road. The Bultmanns' happy mood abated; there is no place for cheerfulness when one catches sight of the misery in this district of Baluchistan. In the 125,000-square-mile area of the provinces Quetta and Kalat live 1.1 million human beings, many of them nomads. Now the quartet of travellers saw the consequences of an annual natural catastrophe. Overturned automobiles and oxcarts lay in the mud and water, the poor possessions of the villagers floated on the flood; for the Indus had once again overrun its banks. The unfortunates accepted their tragedy with apathy, and the grey-veiled heavens wept copiously without pity for the grief they brought.

The road out of Quetta went over mountains. About every ten minutes the two-car caravan was halted at a heavily-armed military post, and passports examined. They were told that caution was imperative, that gangs of bandits made the area unsafe for travellers. Eventually the mountains lay behind them, the desert stretched before them. The road became a mere beaten track, the underlay like a ribbon of corrugated iron with only a few inches between the grooves. They were compelled to slow to about thirty-five miles an hour in order to make any progress at all.

What seemed difficult then, was ideal in comparison with what came later. Problems began to crop up, especially for the Bultmanns. Their Mercedes went on strike—a tyre puncture. Nothing could be easier to set right, thought the practical Däniken. Only: 'We can't change it, we don't have a spare tyre.' EvD looked up at heaven, imploring all the gods. 'How can that be?'

'We started out with three, but we traded them all for souvenirs.' Reason: from Germany all the way to Pakistan they'd never had a flat tyre.

The ever-practical Däniken had yet another solution. From his well-stocked spare parts chest he produced a spray-can which squirted quick-drying liquid rubber into the inner tube. Everything seemed to be going well again. The Bultmanns' Mercedes raced off, and Däniken aimed his Range Rover at the dustcloud behind it.

The trouble had been overcome too easily. Scarcely twenty minutes later the two Swiss found themselves awaited with hopefulness. Now the Mercedes had *two* flats, two disabled tyres, the right front and the left rear. The rubber spray-can was exhausted, and it was still 75 miles to the Iranian border. They were in the middle of the Kandahar desert, in glowing heat.

EvD did what he could. He jacked up the car in order to remove the two wheels. The front one came off easily, but he broke his lug wrench on the rear wheel. He consoled the Germans. He and Willi would take the wheel, find a garage in the border town Taftan, have the tyre repaired and return with professional help for the other tyre. They left the stranded pair some food and everything drinkable. Erich pressed his gas-pistol into Bultmann's hand, showed him how to use it, and was on his way with Dünnenberger.

In Taftan came disillusionment; no repair shop, no help. They must go further, over the Iranian border to Zahedan, 50 miles away. And Willi's temperature started to climb—the thermometer showed 38.9°C (102°F). His chief realised the probable cause: dust-allergy.

At last Zahedan was reached. First, to the nearest hotel by the quickest route. Bathe, shave, change clothing. The feverish Dünnenberger fell into bed, and Däniken filled him up with antibiotics and vitamins and poured hot tea after them.

His civilised appearance regained, EvD took a taxi and made the rounds of all the garages in town. He begged for help, waved bribes, and received friendly responses everywhere. Except that no one was about to drive out into the Pakistan desert where the Bultmanns were stuck. They could not and would not leave Iranian territory.

Däniken was greatly perturbed. It was clear that he himself would have to drive the long road back to help the stranded couple. In spite of his fever, Willi wanted to go with him. Suddenly the telephone rang; on the line: Mrs Bultmann. Five French youngsters in a van had repaired the Bultmanns' tyres and the pair had been able to cross the border. Not much further, unfortunately—another pair of flats. A compassionate Pakistani had brought the wife to Zahedan.

From here on everything went well. Däniken hurried to a garage, bought four tubes and two tyres, and slipped the garageman a 2000-rial bribe to drive with Mrs Bultmann into the desert without delay. Back to her resolute husband.

This was a small episode in a long journey. It was irrelevant to Däniken's project, expended time, nerves and stamina, and had cost 24,000 rials—over 800 German marks.

But doesn't this Samaritan-like behaviour refute the malicious tirades about 'miserly Däniken'? This narration is no attempt to 'rehabilitate' the god-seeker. There is nothing to explain away, because Erich has always been like that, as a child and later as a youth. Examples? Of course!

At fourteen, Erich was a student at the College of Saint-Michel in

Fribourg. A strict father had entered both him and his older brother Otto in the boarding-school. Newly-arrived among strange schoolmates, the lad soon had an opportunity to prove himself. One of the students was in a fix; he had forgotten his exercise-book in the study hall, and the Latin lesson was about to begin. It was too late to fetch the book—the Abbot was already approaching. A fitting punishment was unavoidable.

The Abbot entered the classroom—and was appalled! Blood ran from the mouth of the student Däniken. It welled over his lips and dripped down onto his hands, generating an exciting effect. There was no objection from the teacher as the boy bolted from the room. No sooner was he in the corridor than Däniken dashed to the study hall, stuck the missing Latin book under his shirt, rinsed out his mouth under a water tap and returned to the classroom. There he surreptitiously passed the notebook containing the assigned lesson under the bench to his comrade. No one had noticed anything remarkable about the trick the 14-year-old had played in order to rescue his classmate.

Since childhood days EvD had worn an upper plate. Nobody in the college knew about it, which fact allowed him to carry out his plan. He had furtively removed the plate, and with his own lower teeth bitten his upper gums so forcefully that the blood began to flow. Later in the washroom he had simply replaced the plate and—smiling innocently—returned to the classroom. From that day on he was held in the highest esteem by his classmates. He also acquired a nickname at that time: 'Papa'.

After three years, his father withdrew him from Saint-Michel ostensibly because of business reverses. It can be stated candidly that business was not the only reason; the study of Latin was not exactly one of Däniken's strong points. From my own school experiences, I can feel for him.

An apprentice opening was subsequently sought for the youth, and one was found at the Hotel Schweizerhof in Bern. The previous summer months Erich spent at Lake Sarner, an enthusiastic Boy Scout. As shortly before he had successfully completed a course in Scoutmastership at Magglingen, he was promoted to a position as the camp's organiser and treasurer.

'Papa' Erich had collected still another nickname, 'Guardian Beaver', and belonged to a camp clique of especially close friends. Papa was at everyone's service—a father confessor as well as an organisational genius. It was due to him that camp meals were served promptly; he even acted as unofficial *sous-chef*, tasting various dishes and spicing them with appropriate condiments—the first test-experiments of his future gastronomic career.

The clique consisted of four boys, Papa, Pochi, Unke and 'Bear'. Däniken inclined especially toward the latter; he has always had a liking for the helpless. EvD knew Bear's home well, as he had once stayed overnight in the attic apartment, located directly over the tiny woolshop kept by Bear's mother. The business didn't appear too prosperous, and Erich knew that the woman must work hard to raise money for her son's schooling.

Each day before lunch mail was distributed at the camp. Bear seldom got letters, but on this day his mother had written. The lad withdrew into a quiet corner, and didn't reappear. Not even for lunch, although he'd got his nickname on the basis of his voracious appetite.

Papa was apprehensive, and sought out his friend. Wordlessly he was handed the letter from home. The building owner had given Bear's mother notice to vacate immediately, as rent had not been paid on the date it was due. Besides the threat of eviction, Bear's continued schooling was also in question. Where could the needed money be raised? Däniken promised to help, although at that moment he knew not how. But during the siesta, while he was attending to his duties as camp treasurer, the idea struck him.

He cleaned out the cash-box and passed the money to his friend. With this small sum, the overdue rent would at least be paid. Of course, Bear knew nothing of the source of the funds. He sent his mother a postal money order, and wrote her happily that Erich had helped them out of the fix.

The matter didn't remain secret for long. At first Däniken put off payment to the store-keepers where he purchased the Scout camp's food supplies, promising solemnly to settle the bills later. Then, in his confused and hopeless state, he made off with a packet of banknotes the camp custodian had carelessly left on a table.

The theft exploded—but EvD told the investigating magistrate that he'd lost the missing money from the camp treasury. Fifteen years later, at an 'inquisition' trial in Chur, the sins of his youth would return to haunt him. Not until then did Däniken's friend learn the way in which 'Papa' Erich had rescued him and his mother from their precarious situation. Bear wrote a belated letter of thanks which EvD read in his narrow cell, not without emotion.

Theo Bos, Däniken's Dutch friend, also places a high value on

Däniken's readiness to offer help. They earned their living together around 1960 on the SS *Ryndam*, a liner making the Atlantic crossing between New York and Rotterdam. At that time the 18-year-old Bos, now a 35-year-old Zürich bank employee, was a bellboy on the *Ryndam*, shuttling mail and telegrams to and from the message centre. Between times he brought the stewards coffee, and thus became acquainted with Däniken. He is moved by those fond memories, in which his old friend Erich plays a prominent role.

Bos doesn't deny the misgivings he brought to a reunion with EvD years later, after the latter had become a universally-lionised author. Not that the god-seeker's character had changed, but *something* about him was different. The Netherlander felt this intuitively, and there are few others in such a good position to make comparisons between the old Däniken and the one of today.

'Before,' he said, 'Erich was quite generous and open. To be sure, he's still like that today, but in those days he was also *carefree*, and now that quality seems to be lacking. He gave whatever he had, he helped where it was needed, never asking "Why?" or "What for?" He was that way not only to me, but towards anyone and everyone. Always he thought things through earnestly, involved himself completely in another's problem and tried somehow to help him—with a letter, a conversation or a telephone call.'

He always strove to think himself *into* other persons, said Theo Bos, who was by no means always in complete accord with his friend then. 'Sometimes he became friendly with really impossible types—yet he took care of them, tried constantly to help them. Certainly, he also searched out those he could converse with; but he never did any of this in the style of a benefactor, putting on a big show with his money. Indeed, Erich had none. A hundred francs, that was a lot; fifty francs was the average; ten francs, the usual.'

Faint regret tinges his words as Bos compares those days with nowadays. With that tiny ten-franc capital and a half-hour's energy, Erich could accomplish so much to solve a fellow-man's problems, Bos said. For him too, Erich was the 'Papa'. Then what was different, what had changed?

'Erich always trusted people. His trust for others was absolute. If someone told him something and it rang honestly and sounded reasonable, Erich believed him. Erich was never mistrustful then. Today perhaps, to people who don't know him well, he gives the same impression. But his style is closer to that of a man who says, "Not to worry,

I have enough money. Do you wish fifty, or even a hundred francs from me? Here, it's yours." But this is a different Erich, another man. Erich has become more aware of consequences, and much harder, too. It's clear he has but little time, almost none at all—but in those days that was also true. When Erich took an interest in someone, it was completely, with his entire energy. Today of course he still concerns himself with the troubles and worries of other people, but his concern is much briefer, more subdued, more superficial. . . .'

Do these words sound like the nostalgic reminiscences of a former friend who has somehow become a stranger to the Däniken of today? Or has the Swiss—a man in daily contention with the world that surrounds him—actually changed? Bos believes: 'The trial and the imprisonment have put their mark on him. He's no longer the same man he once was. He isn't as *open* as he was before his bitter experience, understandably.'

Däniken's present reserve, his carefully guarded reactions, did not develop by chance. As Utermann said, 'Anyone who takes the trouble can draw Erich out like a Christmas goose. . . .' He is correct. EvD has been fleeced several times by so-called 'good friends'. His secretary Dünnenberger remembers an especially glaring example.

'There was a young man—let's call him X—who worked for an agency which arranged theatre and lecture tours, Erich's among them. Erich thus became acquainted with him. Moreover, he was a quite speedy and efficient tour manager, which impressed Erich immensely.

'One day as X was leaving the agency, Däniken offered him sole responsibility in organising several European guest-appearances for him. The young man accepted immediately, and in fact everything he scheduled went off perfectly. But when the time came to settle accounts (the tour had indeed been a success), Erich found himself holding an empty bag. It turned out that his generous and high-living friend had been just as generous with the receipts, turning them to his own private use.

'There was a violent quarrel. Erich revoked the exclusive contract, and threatened legal action if X didn't repay the misappropriated money within a specific time.'

Whether the repayment was ever made, Dünnenberger couldn't say with certainty. He did say that afterward Däniken did not completely drop the young man.

'Somehow,' he supposed, they remained distant friends in spite of everything, meeting again here and there from time to time. Erich

This larger-than-life mural hangs on EvD's living room wall. In most vivid fashion, it embodies Däniken's 'creed': Our Gods came from the Stars! The mural, which depicts a cathedral ceiling where a spaceman hangs suspended, had fascinated EvD from the time he first saw it in a Bern gallery. He had to have it, no matter what the price.

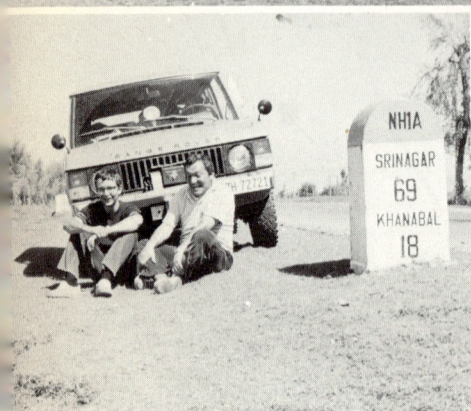

The goal of Däniken's journey to Kashmir in the summer of 1975 was to visit the mysterious Sun – or Hebrew – temple of Srinagar. The hardships of the journey, through flooded areas in Pakistan, plagued by heat and illness, are written on EvD's face in agonising detail (above right). Their strenuous efforts were for a few moments forgotten, however, as the two-man expedition rested, only sixty-nine kilometres from their long-awaited destination.

A vital sequence for the latest Däniken film, *Message of the Gods* is recorded in the house of NASA-engineer Blumrich in Laguna Beach, California. Our photo shows EvD in conversation with film director Harald Reinl.

Orgy in a four-poster? No way . . . EvD's wife need not be upset, it's all innocent fun. Erich von Däniken enjoys playing 'kingpin' occasionally, as he's doing here with 'Bibs' Darlton (left), sister Trudy and editor Utz Utermann, alias Wilhelm Roggersdorf.

When a journey is planned, Däniken's right-hand-man Willi Dünnenberger is always among the party. This young man, who completed a course in business studies, has been EvD's reliable secretary for years. His well-trained 'little grey cells' take care that every move on his boss's complex schedule is made punctually.

At NASA headquarters in Huntsville, Alabama, Erich von Däniken met his friend Josef Blumrich, who has written an engineer's analysis of the Old Testament accounts of the prophet Ezekiel.

Eduardo Chaves made available to EvD a series of interesting photographs which were subsequently published in *My World In Pictures*. EvD returned the kindness in 1975 by inviting the Rio resident to Switzerland.

In 1970 this young man (centre) was EvD's most prominent adversary. 'Anti-Däniken' Gerhard Gadow of West Berlin accused EvD of plagiarism and of using irrelevant source-data.

In August 1974 EvD and Peter Krassa were invited to speak at a lecture hall in Baden – near Vienna. It was filled to bursting point and here, the meeting's organiser, publisher August Breininger (right), is presenting his guests with an honorarium.

The two sceptical-looking gentlemen (foreground) wrote invaluable chapters in Erich von Däniken's success story. ECON publisher Erwin Barth von Wehrenalp (second from right) and editor Utz Utermann (far right) have been deeply involved in the worldwide Däniken-boom.

American sales of Däniken's books have passed the twelve million mark. Few other guest stars can boast of having appeared three times within eight weeks on Johnny Carson's *Tonight* show.

Crazy antics in a smart Salzburg restaurant; the instigator – Erich von Däniken. For those who can't figure out what's going on, be advised that the impulsive Swiss has invented a new form of spiritualistic table-tipping . . .

. . . Of course, as this photo shows, with hands on the floor rather than on the table. Unfortunately, no spirits appeared. © H. Neuper, Salzburg

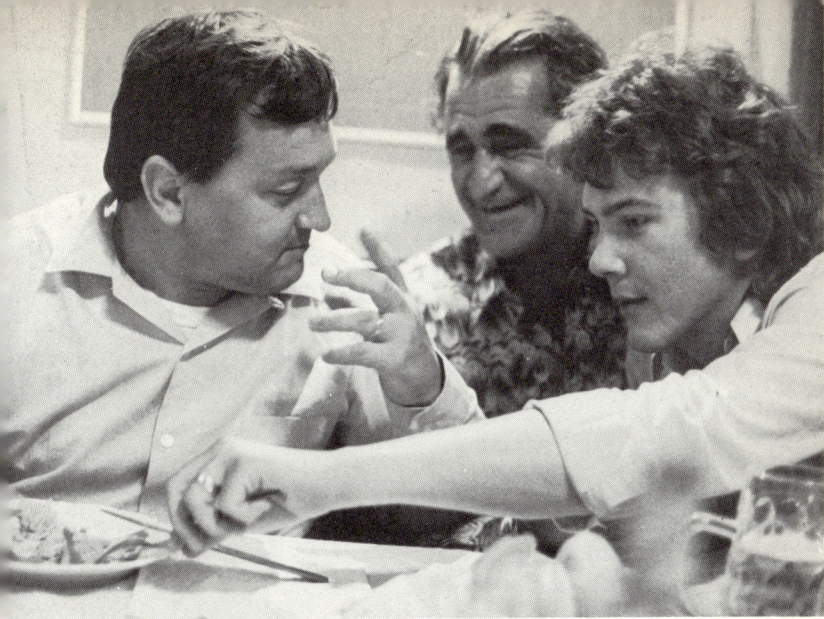

A friendly discussion. Although tolerant of other people's ideas and opinions, Erich von Däniken is not willing to compromise where food is concerned. Here he makes this clear to his friend, Franz Seiner, who is the plate's real owner. Science-fiction author Clark Darlton (centre) is royally amused.   © H. Neuper, Salzburg

Morning gymnastics for the Däniken family.

'Kara ben Däniken' perched high on a camel, dressed in typical Bedouin costume. *Salaam aleikum.*

Däniken and companion Hans Neuner, in Egypt for the first time. They spent three weeks travelling from Cairo to Luxor, Aswan and Abu Simbel; naturally they travelled aboard 'ships of the desert'. Later they continued north to Beirut and Baalbek.

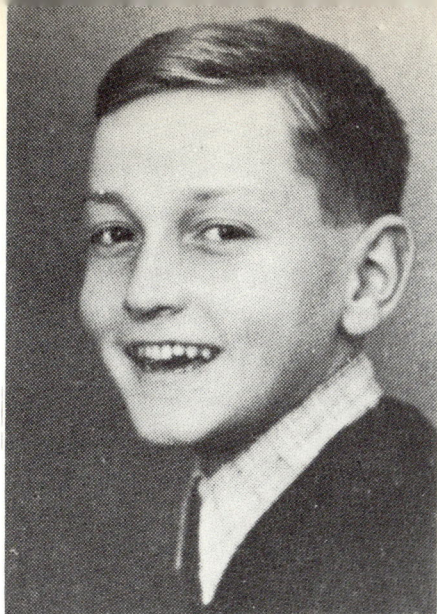

At twelve, Erich was a typical 'young rascal'.

Däniken's talent for organising led him to become a Boy Scout Troopleader. 'Papa' Erich (second from left) and his four best Scout friends.

Slender and wiry, that was EvD at fifteen, a Scout Pathfinder with heart and soul. He was also full of impulsive notions.

Although he scarcely has time to think about holidays, a brief skiing holiday is Däniken's yearly relaxation. Years before he became a famous writer, he skied regularly with his friend Theo Bos (right).

During his early years, EvD tried his hand as a bartender in exclusive hotels and on luxury liners.

Erich von Däniken married his German bride Elisabeth Skaja on 26 November 1960, at Stein-on-the-Rhine. Neither of them could have foreseen what turbulent ups-and-downs the next sixteen years would bring.

Elisabeth von Däniken, called 'Ebet' by her husband, is a loyal companion as well as wife. During 1975 EvD spent only 116 days at his home – one can imagine how he treasures his limited family life. © Neue Revue, Hamburg

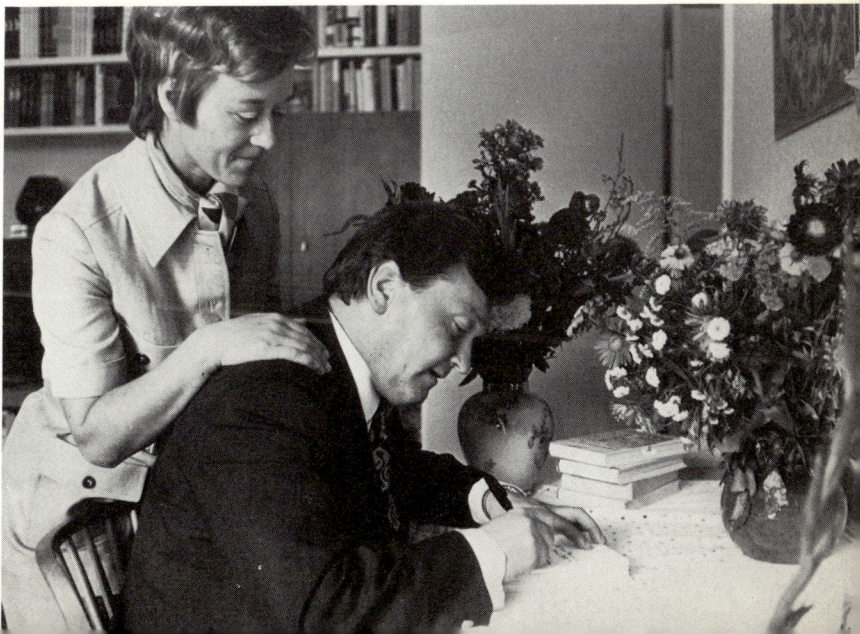

Graphically demonstrated in the garden of his Bonstetten home, here's a hearty 'smack' for the camera, just like a film's happy ending.

Immediately after being kissed, Däniken returns to mapping his itinerary. Elisabeth attentively studies Erich's next God-tracking route.

Too seldom does Däniken find time for relaxed conversation within his own four walls.

© C. Lang, Adliswil

On 13 February 1970, this picture was flashed around the world – Erich von Däniken in the dock.

EvD lets a 'pro' (his brother Otto) initiate him in the art of fishing.

© OLS, Lauf

The prosecutors: examining magistrate Hans-Peter Kirchhofer (right) and district attorney Willy Padrutt.

'In my house I am the master' Erich von Däniken seems to be thinking – and who would dispute it – so loyally guarded by his two dogs. I wouldn't recommend entering into a dispute with giant 'Neptun', and 'Luna', the Highland Terrier, is small indeed, but watch out . . .

© R. Vögtlin, Zürich

still has a certain sympathy for X, even though the incident is not entirely erased from his memory.'

Däniken's wife Elisabeth confirms the fact that such incidents are typical. 'My husband is over-generous, and he values true friendship greatly. I must say that I'm a little stand-offish with several of his friends, perhaps even mistrustful. Obviously, any prominent man has very many so-called "friends". Erich is too easy-going in this respect. He has a spontaneous impulse to help, and is forever possessed by the idea that he has a certain responsibility toward such people. At home we've had endless discussions on this subject.' Mrs von Däniken sighed. 'Eventually these superficial friendships evaporate. Erich himself will never openly admit that I was right; so although this happens over and over again, I just keep silent. It would be futile to say self-righteously, "See—I told you so!" ' Hence, Erich von Däniken's circle of close friends is not over-large.

'I believe Erich has very few really good friends,' says Däniken's secretary who of course is one of this circle. 'The prime reason being that their respective circumstances are so dissimilar. Most of those who call themselves Däniken's friends merely want to gain in some way from the relationship.' Willi Dünnenberger speaks from experience. 'So Erich knows enough to treasure all the more those whose friendship lasts, friends who are not aiming at Däniken's pocket, but who simply like him without reservations or complications.'

Indeed, money and friendship are seldom directly linked. In Däniken's case, however, there is a connection. That may be because the jet-set traveller wants to prove his bond with other human beings—for want of time to develop an amicable link unhurriedly—by reaching deep into his pocketbook. This is not philanthropic pomposity, as one might think. He is simply so—spontaneous and magnanimous.

I remember the autumn of 1973. I was awaiting the imminent appearance of my 'first-born'. Initially scheduled for September, the publishing date of my book *Als die gelben Götter kamen* (*When the Yellow Gods Came*) had been delayed for technical reasons.

So on the spur of the moment I decided, instead of the planned presentation to the media, to arrange a get-to-know-one-another meeting between the author and prominent Vienna booksellers. The date was set for Thursday, September 6, at the Vienna cafe-restaurant 'Laterndlgrill'. I had informed von Däniken of my plans, and learned with great joy that he would also attend.

I proposed to give the booksellers a foretaste of my book in the form of a slide-show. And as man does not live by air alone, I also arranged with the restaurateur to put on an elaborate buffet. It cost some 3500 schillings, and I was able to afford one-third of that as a down payment.

Erich von Däniken came, with him his secretary Dünnenberger, as well as Walter Ernsting. It was a successful evening—but then came time to pay. My motion toward my wallet was intercepted by Däniken. He said only, 'Let it be,' drew a few banknotes from his breast pocket and settled the balance of my bill. He didn't even want to hear my fervent thanks.

A bagatelle for a millionaire, perhaps many would say. Of course! But does that explain his spontaneous action? Wealth is one thing, generosity and readiness to help is another. Däniken knew that 3500 schillings would tear a large hole in my small budget; therefore he came to my aid of his own accord. It was the act of a friend.

I repeat, for EvD friendship is certainly not an empty word. 'He has never left a friend in the lurch,' pronounced Willi Dünnenberger, who knows very well what his employer expects from his friends in return. An open and honest approach is always accepted—he values honest, straightforward people. But he must have the constant feeling that he can depend on them if need be, that to be genuine the friendship must be reciprocal.

Hans Neuner, Däniken's companion on his first voyages abroad, shares this view. 'Erich doesn't call everyone "friend", he draws a very sharp line. The word "friend" always came more easily to my lips than to Erich's.' The Tyrolean, who acquired his gastronomical education from scratch, made Däniken's acquaintance when he was a bartender at Davos's Hotel Europe, where the then-lessee of the Hotel Rosenhügel occasionally drank. That was in 1965.

'You can't say that word "friend" so casually.' EvD once admonished him during a discussion of the concept of friendship. Neuner remembers this conversation as if it were yesterday. 'You must be one hundred per cent convinced about the person in question,' advised EvD, and, 'You must have just as strong a conviction that he would do the same for you as you would for him!' This discussion, says Neuner today, taught him for the first time to differentiate between acquaintances, casual acquaintances, closer acquaintances and genuine friends, 'of which one has few, very few indeed'.

Friendship of a special sort has also developed between Erich von Däniken and his editor Utz Utermann. Originally engaged by ECON-boss Wehrenalp to make Däniken's manuscript more readable—an act which at first encountered EvD's strong disapproval—author and editor are today of a single mind.

'Our relationship is very close,' rejoices Utermann, 'Even when Erich is in the USA, in South America, Canada, Australia or wherever, we keep in constant touch by mail. And also by phone; the telephone administration is in a perpetual state of euphoria over the considerable toll charges!' He philosophised thoughtfully: 'Regarding *friends*, I feel that this precious word is spoken all too lightly nowadays. Should a man find in all his life three friends on whom he can depend unconditionally, then he is richly rewarded. Such a friendship binds Erich and me. Since I first met Erich in 1968, nothing about him has changed. At that time he was weighed down with worries—although I first learned that fact later, while making inquiries for my book *Das seltsame Leben des Erich von Däniken*. His worries were well-concealed; he was imbued with the ideas that he expressed to me, and they simply took precedence over everything.'

Utermann thinks that those few contemporaries who are able to devote themselves so completely to a single idea, belief or endeavour should be cherished as 'living monuments'. He bemoaned the fact that such individuals, great personalities, 'movers and shakers', are almost extinct. On the subject of friendship between men, he set standards. 'It functions only if friends are able to say *anything* to each other. Erich and I can discuss openly both pleasant and unpleasant topics.' And most essential for the preservation of such a friendship, observes Däniken's editor, is the presence of humour. 'Humour, that's the cornerstone; humour that isn't at another's expense, but that may occasionally be turned back upon oneself. This sort of humour Erich has in unlimited quantity.' He, Utermann, could in no circumstances ever be friends with anyone who didn't possess a measure of humour. 'A man must be able instantly to stand back and have a good look at himself. Erich can do that.'

Utz Utermann (he's carried the nickname 'Utz' since school days) remembers fondly the hours they worked together. Unfortunately, not much time is available for literary co-production, as Däniken is travelling for the greater part of the year. During the few weeks of his 'holidays at home' time is set aside to finish and polish the latest manuscript. This is done alternately in Bonstetten or Roggersdorf.

'But even when we're working hard,' qualifies Utermann 'there's always enough time for a hearty laugh in-between—sometimes so hearty that the walls shake. Intensive work, certainly, but now and then it drags, right in the middle. Slavish devotion to labour, that we don't have.'

This teamwork is naturally productive, for over the years Utermann and Däniken have achieved a splendid balance in their work together. Often, when one of them begins a sentence, the other knows exactly how it should be completed. 'Were it necessary,' says Utermann, 'we could even converse in ciphers.'

Such an intellectual bond between two persons is not uncommon. Walter Ernsting felt a similar rapport upon first meeting Däniken. There had been an initial exchange of letters, and then on July 16, 1968 —just before EvD's last journey before his Vienna arrest—their first face-to-face encounter. Ernsting, today: 'I still remember it perfectly. Erich arrived in an ancient, rattling, blue-grey Volkswagen, one he had rented. I was living in Salzburg then. We greeted each other like old friends, although our short acquaintance till then rested solely on an exchange of two friendly letters.'

Ernsting attributed this instantly-felt harmony to 'the similarity of thoughts and concepts' which gave substance to that first impression, solidifying their personal relationship at the outset. He values EvD as a good, true and reliable friend, and believes retrospectively that, 'Erich was delighted to meet someone who thought as he did.' In all these years, there is one signal conclusion among many that Ernsting has made: Erich keeps his promises. 'Very seldom does he promise anything. But when he does, one can depend upon it absolutely!'

Once, in 1975, I telephoned Erich for some compelling reason. At the end of our conversation he said, 'It must have cost you a heap of piastres to phone me here in Bonstetten. Next time I see you, you'll get a hundred francs from me.' 'That's not at all necessary,' I said, honestly trying to dissuade him; but he insisted on it.

Our next meeting occurred months later in Munich. I said not a word about the hundred francs, but waited tautly for him to bring up the subject. In vain. It appeared that his promise was forgotten. Then in January 1976, on Epiphany, Däniken flew to Vienna for a day. We met, gossiped, conversed about various things—and suddenly my visitor reached into his briefcase, pulled out a hundred-franc note and slapped it on the table. I looked on astounded. 'What's that for?'

'I promised you over the phone that I'd pay you 100 francs for your telephone expenses. Don't you remember?'

More than six months had elapsed, but Däniken had kept his promise.

So many who know him make much of his gratitude. I can corroborate that, too. When *Als die gelben Götter kamen* finally did appear, my Munich publisher held a press-reception in a Chinese restaurant. As EvD had written the Foreword, I thought it appropriate to invite him to Munich too. He came. In addition to several journalists a reporter from Southwest-Radio-Stuttgart also showed up. He recorded a joint interview with von Däniken and me. The unavoidable question came up.

'Mr von Däniken, why did you bother to write a foreword for Peter Krassa? For a man with your notoriety and fame, it was certainly not necessary." Däniken's reply came without hesitation. "Look, during *my* difficult time Peter, in his role as an objective journalist, gave me a little help. Now I'm helping *him*!'

He has done that, and more than once. Here is another example: EvD called my first book to the attention of Bantam Books, probably the world's largest publisher of paperbacks. They were interested and acquired the rights; *When the Yellow Gods Came* will soon appear in America. This good deed of intercession will not profit him one penny—he has categorically refused to accept any payment. Would any other competing author act this way? Remember, Bantam is the very same giant book-factory which has published four of his five books, with printings totalling 13 million copies. (A sixth book, *Beweise* (*Proofs*) has not yet appeared in English at the time of writing.)

For him, friendship is not an empty word, and loyalty is a necessary corollary of friendship. EvD is a man of sensitivity, even though his outward appearance seems to contradict this characteristic, Däniken glows with energy, is heavy-set with broad shoulders, sturdy back, rather short legs, strong arms and hands that know what work means. He isn't tall, perhaps slightly over five feet six; yet strangely, when he stands among physically taller people (and this is the case more often than not), one does *not* get the impression that he is a shorter man. Däniken's figure dominates the scene.

'Most striking are Erich's unbelievably warm and sparkling eyes.' NASA-engineer Josef Blumrich tells of his impressions upon first meeting the god-seeker. Their correspondence began in January, 1971, but they shook hands for the first time in March of 1972 in Huntsville, where Blumrich still lived and worked. (He is now on a pension and settled in California.)

The Austrian rocket-builder found in Däniken a kindred soul, though he has to laugh when he thinks of this first encounter. 'The whole man was constantly in motion. It's flat-out impossible to photo-graph him—I've been unable to obtain a reasonably good photo so far. His face, his hands, every part of him is incessantly animated. Däniken is a ball of concentrated energy.

But he is also a sort of seismograph which reacts to moods and dispositions. Perhaps this is the reason he is so receptive to a genuine, honestly-intended friendship. He gives his unconditional trust to anyone who stands by him.

One of these few is Theo Bos, friend from the old days. 'Friendship,' says he, 'means for Erich and me loyalty and above all, honesty. Honesty in a very broad sense. Honest in everything you say to each other, in statements about emotions or weaknesses. Who confesses to a friend that he's weak, that sometimes he's given to weeping? That he likes to spend money, or that he never has the courage to start any-thing new? I believe that the confession of weakness—in the sexual area perhaps, or in one's general inability to accomplish this or that—is extremely difficult to talk about at all.'

'Who will admit freely that sometimes he feels very much alone, even though he knows many people and appears to have fifty friends or more? Discussing such subjects with an intimate is evidence of true friendship.'

As stated earlier, Theo Bos gained EvD's friendship long before the Swiss globetrotter rose to world fame. Bos came to know him 'unadulterated'. He reminisces:

'When we bellboys first learned that Erich was Swiss, we decided among ourselves that he must be an expert yodeller. One day we got up nerve enough to ask him to yodel for us. Like the good fellow he is, he promised he would. A few days later he came to our tiny cabin.

'He stood and composed himself for a moment, then emitted a stone-dissolving yodel. It was a severe shock for us. We naïve flatland Dutchmen had believed that a yodel must be joyful, should hint at the romance and adventure of the high Alps. But Erich just stood there and *shouted* his yodel, permeating the cabin. It wasn't beautiful at all, just loud.'

Yet Theo Bos admired the Swiss steward for other reasons. After all, Däniken spoke several languages effortlessly—English, French, Italian, Dutch and German (the three-tongued Swiss be thanked)—while besides his mother-tongue, bellboy Bos could only mangle a few words of broken English.

'When it was necessary, Erich was even able to make himself understood in Spanish and Portuguese. Because of his ability with languages he was eventually singled out to work in the lounge during afternoon tea, where he had to give messages and make multi-lingual announcements over the public address system. We bellboys looked up to him, and ran to serve him coffee whenever he wanted it.

'I think at first I was so struck by Erich that I sometimes startled him unintentionally. Once I'd brought him some coffee, and returned a half-hour later to pick up the empty cup. I noticed that it wasn't quite empty, and asked in my stumbling German, 'Warum hast du deinen Kaffee noch nicht ausgesauft?' (Why haven't you *swilled* up your coffee?) His instantaneous reaction was to pick up an ice-bucket and invert it over my head. A bitterly-cold and wet experience.'

My first encounter with EvD in person was in Trieste in July of 1972. Three friends and I set out for the Italian film-metropolis in a decrepit old automobile. Not for the purpose of meeting Däniken, but to attend the science-fiction film festival held there each summer. The entire undertaking was bootless, though we could have used rubber boots for it rained and blew for six days of the eight-day festival; only the first and the last day were dry.

We were camping in Sistiana, and at night I held fast to the tent stakes for fear that the unceasing storm would sweep us away. Our treasury was melting away like butter in the (absent!) sun: petrol coupons were not cheap, and the camp ground was over 20 kilometres from Trieste. We drove back and forth over this short but crooked stretch twice daily, to attend both the day and evening screenings. As most of the films being shown were of but middling quality, the sole benefit I accrued from this journey was a completely unexpected rendezvous with my some time pen-pal Däniken.

EvD had flown in from Zürich to see the film 'Silent Running'. We didn't have much time then to get really acquainted, but it was nevertheless an electrifying first encounter. A few weeks later in Salzburg we met again at Walter Ernsting's home, and EvD spontaneously addressed me using the informal pronoun 'thou'. It was said as naturally as if we had known each other for years.

Perhaps that is Däniken's real recipe for success, the automatic, unaffected acceptance of nominal strangers. He is entirely without presumption, lacks all deviousness, and adjusts himself with relative ease to any new situation or environment. To be like that, an ingrained knowledge of human nature is surely necessary. EvD has it. Moreover, in the years from 1968 to 1971 he had ample opportunity to learn by experience—in prison. I believe that today he knows instinctively whom he can trust, on whom he can depend. Additionally, he knows how to take control of unpleasant situations with instinctive skill and by the use of solemn gravity.

One such situation occurred on September 10, 1973, in Berlin's Theater des Westens, while Däniken was presenting a slide-lecture on the theme 'Were the Gods Astronauts?'

The god-seeker's usual practice was first to give the whole lecture and show the accompanying slides, and then allow time for his audience to ask questions and discuss relevant problems with him and among themselves.

In the beginning it seemed to be going the same way in Berlin. I was sitting in the first balcony, and soon realised that almost all the seats around me were occupied by vociferous students, identifiable by an overheard word or two as being from the Free University of Berlin. One of them especially, a blond-maned lad on my left, apparently didn't have the patience to hold his witticisms until the lecture ended. He jumped up suddenly, leaned over the railing and called theatrically to Däniken: 'G-e-n-a-u-e-r e-r-k-l-ä-r-e-n, l-a-n-g-s-a-m-e-r s-p-r-e-c-h-e-n, b-e-s-s-e-r d-e-f-i-n-i-e-r-e-n!' (Explain more clearly, speak slower, define it better!)

The lecturer paused, looked up at his heckler and said unperturbedly with the same intonation: 'K-o-m-m-t s-c-h-o-n, Z-e-i-t- l-a-s-s-e-n, b-e-s-s-e-r m-a-c-h-e-n!' (Coming soon, allow time, it improves!) For a moment the auditorium was silent, then a storm of laughter and applause broke out: Däniken had won the round. The blond-maned one was not heard from again. Ready wit coupled with a knowledge of human nature are Däniken's trump cards.

Utermann has yet another plus for the god-seeker. 'Erich cannot live without music—he has both a taste and a knack for it. I'll bet if someone sent him into the forest with an unfamiliar instrument, Erich would return a half-hour later, playing it!' Utermann deems this musical bent to be 'an intrinsic element of the international success Däniken's lectures have enjoyed'. EvD is a polyglot. It doesn't daunt him one bit to stand before microphones and television cameras in various lands. Ke knows that his linguistic ability will see him through anywhere.

There's another example of EvD's fine-tuned ear; it's somehow typical of the man himself. At a press conference in New York a journalist completely unknown to him stood up and asked a question.

Erich responded promptly: 'If I'm not mistaken,' he said to the news-man, 'you're of Italian descent. Would you rather I answered in Italian?' The man addressed was taken aback. Born in America and living in New York's Italian quarter, he nevertheless believed he spoke American English with no trace of an accent. But Erich—and this is surely indicative of his musical ear—had spotted the man's ancestry immediately. In this connection another item occurs to me, an intro-ductory sentence Erich uses to open most of his American lectures: 'Ladies and gentlemen, please excuse my poor English—I'm right in the process of acquiring my fifth language.'

Sly, isn't it? In one sentence Erich has indeed confessed his weakness, but balanced it with an advantage—his linguistic skill. He has made two points: his audience is prepared to allow for any of the speaker's blunders, but is also impressed by Däniken's seemingly casually-dropped remark that he speaks four languages.

EvD realised and began to indulge his love of music in his early years. Even at the strict College of Saint-Michel he founded a jazz band, in which he himself played trumpet. Last March I was a witness to my friend's unpublicised talent. Däniken had come to Vienna to join me in a book-autographing appearance. In the evening the three of us, EvD, Walter Ernsting and I visited the well-known Viennese club Jazzland. Däniken was greeted enthusiastically, hoisted onto the stage and urged to give the audience a musical morsel.

The room was jammed. A spotlight was focused on the guest, who needed no further incentive. Däniken sat down at the piano, started tapping the keys, and extemporaneously hammered out a competent boogie-woogie. The audience, jazz-buffs all, roared. When we'd entered the place, a band was in full swing. One of the group now handed Erich his trumpet and entreated him to play a solo, but Däniken firmly refused. He hadn't played this instrument for years, and couldn't play without first practising a bit.

He made amends by growling a hoarse chorus of the St Louis Blues à la Louis Armstrong, wildly supported by the inspired band. The atmosphere in the club was charged with elation—the unexpected impromptu act had added something electric to the evening's show. This swinging Däniken was an undreamt-of extra attraction.

I've already said it: our Swiss has a sure instinct for certain situations. Former schoolmates can attest to EvD's extraordinary intelligence. At fourteen he was already well-read—although the type of literature young Erich devoured surreptitiously was not the type recommended, or even permitted, by his school. Saint-Michel was a traditionally strict Catholic institution. But EvD read such 'satanic' books as—one can well imagine—Nietzsche's *The Antichrist*. From that time on, Däniken's Christian conception of the world has remained severely shaken. He does not deny his critical distance from the Church, maintained by knowledge gathered from his own experiences.

In May 1975, Däniken and I visited Bern Cathedral. A magnificently carved relief is displayed over the entrance. It is a representation of the Last Judgment. Above, on a canopied throne: the Trinity; on the right, the saved; to the left, the damned. I couldn't abstain from murmuring a needling remark. 'One day you're going to be found standing there on the left,' said I to my companion.

Däniken looked at me, laughed, and dryly replied: 'Not at all— I'll be sitting on the throne!'

CHAPTER V

Was Däniken a Plagiarist?

Successful people must count on an inevitable consequence of success—
the advent of enemies and adversaries. Erich von Däniken, one of the
most successful, had and has them in full measure. His intriguing ideas
provoke the envious and incite the narrow-minded. The latter chal-
lenge him, the former write detailed refutations. Books and articles
about him and his theories spring up like mushrooms in Europe and
elsewhere. Less successful authors are inspired to write books like
Gerschäfte mit der Phantasie (*The Business of Fantasy*), and at the going
rate for defamation.

Gilbert A. Bourquin, editor of the Swiss magazine *Blick*, and Sergius
Golowin, the country's unofficial specialist in popular folklore, collaborated on a so-called 'vindication' of the French writer Robert
Charroux. This was done under the sponsorship of the German publishing house Herbig, which had previously published two of
Charroux's books, although with moderate sales success. The jet take-
off of Erich von Däniken, whose first book quickly rose to the top of
the best-seller lists, made his competitors nervous. What should be
done? Bourquin and Golowin knew. In their book *The Däniken Story*
they accused EvD of misappropriating the substance of Charroux's
ideas and publishing them as his own. They went on to hurl at Däniken
every possible slander inventive minds could devise.

Fribourg theologian Othmar Keel-Leu took a different tack. In his
booklet *Zurück von den Sternen* (*Return from the Stars*), he gave full
rein to his indignation over Däniken's 'heretical' interpretation of the
Old Testament.

But the greatest stir was caused by the first publication of an 18-
year-old student at the Free University of Berlin. First published
privately, *Erinnerungen an die Wirklichkeit* was reprinted as a Fischer

paperback. What the young author, Gerhard Gadow, aimed to show in his polemic was spelled out in the foreword, in which he regretted that,

> Unfortunately it was not possible to investigate thoroughly all of the 'unsolved mysteries of the past' mentioned by Däniken; for to track down mainly erroneous, occasionally false and seldom accurate source-references for his assertions would have required years of investigation. . . .

And a few lines later:

> This manuscript is not composed with the perhaps necessary objectivity. Its controversial character is undeniable. . . .

In the mass media, which devoted an extraordinary amount of attention to his book, Gadow was dubbed 'Anti-Däniken'. In just a few months his *Memories of Actuality* sold about 85,000 copies. He spoke on radio talk-shows and made guest appearances on television, gave lectures and discussed his dissertation on demand.

The person most affected couldn't avoid for long taking notice of his adversary. Their first meeting was at a public debate in North Germany in October 1971 after Däniken's release from prison. Gadow had charged the god-seeker, in spite of the extensive list of source-references quoted in *Erinnerungen*, with extracting the bulk of his information from five books:

—*Aufbruch ins Dritte Jahrtausend* (*Morning of the Magicians*) by Jacques Bergier and Louis Pauwels.

—*Phantastische Vergangenheit* and *Verratene Geheimnisse* by Robert Charroux.

—*Gods, Graves and Scholars* by C. W. Ceram.

—*History of Life and Death* by Francis Bacon.

What Gadow resented was the fact that Däniken didn't mention any of the listed works nor their authors in the text of his book. One could search in vain for Ceram's book in EvD's bibliography, and mention of Charroux's *Verratene Geheimnisse* appeared only in later editions, after Herbig protested to ECON. By the use of tables, the Berlin 'Anti-Däniken' attempted to prove that Däniken's inspirations were formulated by Pauwels and Bergier. Namely, Gadow wanted it realised that *Morning of the Magicians* was the actual source 'from which Däniken had drawn copiously'. Putting it baldly, he said that the one had simply plagiarised the other.

What reasons did Gerhard Gadow have for composing his polemic?

'There were several motives for writing my Däniken-book,' the young author stated retrospectively, 'the main one being the Berlin Science-Fiction Club's intensive occupation with this theme around the turn of the year 1968–9. Lively discussions went on for several nights running, and I remarked that many of those taking part lacked the special knowledge necessary to judge or criticise various vital questions. And as I could easily imagine how many other discussion groups suffered from this same deficiency, I wanted to compile a collection of material on the theme, simultaneously expressing my own opinions.'

Gadow asserts that he doesn't have a negative attitude toward Däniken's hypotheses, 'anyway, not in the sense that I hold his theories to be impossibilities'. But he considers the credibility of Däniken's circumstantial evidence to be another matter. Now as before the Berliner maintains the same posture towards Däniken's evidence: 'That which I have taken time to check thoroughly does not convince me.'

These reproaches, that he has stolen from other authors and unethically adopted their ideas as his own, Erich von Däniken does not allow to go unchallenged. He says he first came to read Charroux's book *Phantastische Vergangenheit* at a time when his own manuscript of *Erinnerungen* had long been lying on the desk of an ECON reader. And publisher von Wehrenalp calls upon Charroux himself as the star witness in refuting the accusations. 'I have a copy of a statement written by Charroux in which he says':

> May I affirm anew that I do not hold the view that author Erich von Däniken has plagiarised me in his book *Erinnerungen*. . . . It is true that certain channels of thought are similar, yet that can only be attributed to an inevitable convergence which I cannot equate with plagiarism. I have no intention of bringing an action against Mr von Däniken; on the contrary, I would most strongly oppose such an undertaking should it be initiated by others. I hope that this episode, begun in a misleading press campaign, is concluded on the basis of this official statement.

Charroux's first two books were published in German by Herbig Press. A Dr Herbert Fleissner, attempting to bring a charge of plagiarism against ECON through Charroux's French publisher Robert Laffont, was bitterly disappointed. Monsieur Laffont answered him on

March 12, 1969, that the firm's attorneys had read the (French) translation of *Erinnerungen* and were of the opinion that it contained no essential fact on which to base a legal action. '. . . for if Däniken let himself be inspired by certain thoughts and disclosures of Charroux, he did so, as did Charroux, in the role of reporter; and while he leaned upon already-known hypotheses, he offered his own personal conclusions. Charroux had earlier done the same with Pauwels-Bergier's *Aufbruch . . .*' appended Laffont placatingly.

Of course at that time he knew something which Dr Fleissner did not—exactly why the requested war-cry against ECON should not be let loose. He already had in his pocket a contract to publish the French translation of Däniken's best-selling first-born, and had not the slightest interest in starting a quarrel with EvD's publisher. Three years later another work of Charroux's appeared in German translation—not published by Herbig, however, but by Däniken's publisher ECON.

Gadow's polemic didn't pass unnoticed at Wehrenalp's headquarters in Düsseldorf, but nobody panicked. Almost with aloofness, the ECON-boss says today: 'Naturally we read Gadow's Anti-Däniken brochure *Erinnerungen an die Wirklichkeit*. With equanimity, as a matter of fact. We had set up an "Erich von Däniken" bureau, headed by an academician, to follow up each source and to assemble all attacks and refutations. After sifting through this material and discovering that many of Däniken's opponents were unavailable for further comment, we decided not to take these attacks too seriously.'

Däniken's editor Utermann accentuated even more clearly the absurdity of Gadow's charges of plagiarism. He was asked whether any of the material was lifted from Pauwels-Bergier or Charroux.

'Certainly not, and I found these charges ridiculous from the start. Look, for me the editing and rewriting was merely one job among many others. I knew nothing of the specific subjects dealt with—I just took the raw text and reworked it, including polishing away all the Swiss-isms. Speaking categorically, I added no new concepts. From where should I have taken them? It comes down to this: for the reasons mentioned, scarcely a passage of the original text remained unchanged.

'So in the event the reproaches were valid, that Erich borrowed from or simply removed another's ideas, ESP-phenomena must have been involved. For if similar conclusions were drawn, they evolved from the exact same sources utilised by all four authors—Pauwels, Bergier, Charroux and Däniken. I myself first read the books of the three

French writers a good year after submission of the Däniken manuscript, namely at the time these mind-blowing accusations were made.'

In spite of the spirited debate between the Swiss author and his Berlin opponent, it wasn't until spring of 1974 that the two quarrelsome adversaries became better acquainted. Significantly, the initiative came from Däniken, who invited Gadow to accompany him on a lecture tour through the United States and Canada. EvD has a strong inclination to study closely people who especially interest him, including those whose opinions differ from his. He simply wants to know *why* someone is opposed to him, to analyse the other's reasons and incentives—and he is usually successful in doing so. Of course Gerhard Gadow is not 'just anybody'. On the contrary, his character is rather singular. He is unusually reserved, mistrustful perhaps, a man who attempts to conceal his inner self from the world around him. It may be that he feels himself judged unfairly, but I can only depict him as he appears to me, face to face. This took place in September 1973 during a stay in Berlin. The occasion was a conference of the Science-Fiction Club—mentioned earlier by Gadow—to which Erich von Däniken and I had both been invited.

I was somewhat curious about the Berlin 'Anti-Däniken', our acquaintanceship thus far having been limited to a single exchange of letters. Now as he entered the room, a medium-tall young man with almost expressionless features and deliberately distant attitude, he gave a clearly perceptible impression of—inaccessibility. No smile flickered across his face, every word he spoke seemed to be programmed; unaffectedness was wholly lacking. What was especially irritating to me at this first encounter—although we were engaged in direct conversation, Gadow constantly looked *past* me.

It's clear to me today that EvD's opponent was heavily laden with complexes, as every person is to a lesser extent. He had—not only then—an almost sensual compulsion to show up Däniken as being absurd. On this September evening Gadow used every subtlety, down to seemingly unimportant details, to bolster his reputation as the 'Anti-Däniken'. That is his image, a means to obtain not only money—I believe that is secondary—but public recognition. Anyway, these were my impressions of the undoubtedly interesting personality of the young writer Gerhard Gadow.

He obviously pictures himself otherwise. Asked how he would characterise himself, he back-pedals somewhat: 'My image as Anti-Däniken is of much less importance to me than one would perhaps believe. It is important to me that the opinions I defend in my books (Gadow also wrote *Der Atlantis-Streit—The Atlantis Controversy*) turn out to be essentially correct; and in case they do not, that I can and must retract them at the appropriate time. . . .'

Concerning the subject of Däniken's theories and hypotheses, Gadow seems to have stuck by his guns. Asked about this he replied—unimpressed by Däniken's immense readership: 'The pertinent statements in by book *Erinnerungen an die Wirklichkeit* remain unchanged to the same extent as Daniken's books appear to have remained unchanged. I am of course always ready, should factual errors be pointed out to me, to correct these errors in [future editions of] my book.'

On the other hand—especially during their trip to America in autumn of 1974—the radiation of Däniken's personality falling upon Gadow seems to have had some effect. In great contrast to his attempts to refute EvD's theses, the Berliner avoids going into detail.

'About my last get-together with Erich von Däniken I can only state that the impressions I received then were very interesting, and certain vital points were clarified concerning subjects on which I had no accurate views or opinion. I consider the meeting and the journey to have been quite advantageous not only for me but for Erich von Däniken, who has expressed himself similarly.'

No official communiqué following a diplomatic conference could have been worded more nebulously. But had the trip abroad together improved the personal relationship between the two? 'Diplomat' Gadow cautiously keeps his distance: 'My attitude towards Däniken personally has not changed to any great extent, for even before we met it was not well-defined, being based solely on what he had written. Of course it has now solidified through personal impressions of a quite interesting person with many thoroughly charming traits.'

Gadow judged his experience during the American tour as 'positive'. He considered his travelling companion to be a 'personal plus', and could see for himself the tremendous response of people in the USA and Canada to Däniken, evidenced by the sold-out houses wherever EvD lectured on visits of astronaut-gods. Had Gadow any thoughts about the reasons for such success?

'Erich von Däniken's success is due to a combination of several things,' said Gadow, trying to analyse the best-seller phenomenon, 'one vital factor being the date his first book appeared. Moon flights had started, and preparations for a manned moon-landing had kindled public interest. Naturally, the theses that von Däniken presented met with greater receptivity among more elements of the population than before; until then such theories had seldom been discussed, had remained at a low level in public consciousness.'

Gadow didn't want to charge Däniken with using a 'patent recipe', but he of course believes that the way in which each book was presented —in internal structure, in style, even in dimensions—was deliberately calculated for optimum effect on the potential buyer (well, how else!). Thus did EvD finally attain an enormous readership. To be sure, Gadow lays much stress on discriminating the form from the content. In no way does he identify himself with the latter.

He also differentiates between his attitude towards the person Däniken, and towards the credibility of Däniken's theories. 'I have never felt any personal antipathy toward the writer of *Erinnerungen*,' says Gadow today, 'only a great interest in the theme, and an eagerness to adjust my opinions to my present state of knowledge.'

Rumours that the Berlin author will try once more to come to terms with Däniken in a literary sense were denied by Gadow.

'I do not plan in the imminent future to again associate myself publicly with Erich von Däniken. What I had to say about his theories, about individual facts and pseudo-facts, I have already said. For my part, I consider our discussion at an end; however, should new viewpoints surface, I would of course be ready to reflect on them and to change—if it were necessary—opinions I have held up to now.'

CHAPTER VI

Success is no Accident

It's not such a long leap from Däniken the apparent plagiarist to Däniken the successful author, for the good reason that one plainly cancels out the other. In other words, if the god-seeker had really built his worldwide renown upon plagiarism, it would have been the first case to my knowledge where a writer became famous by disseminating an assortment of the better ideas of others as his own. Additionally, it would have been a thoroughly absurd situation if the apparent plagiarist surpassed in popular appeal the author(s) he'd stolen from.

Certainly, Louis Pauwels, Jacques Bergier and Robert Charroux (Däniken's alleged 'inspirational fathers') have been translated into many languages; their books are familiar to all those interested in these themes. But neither the quantity of their published works nor their level of popularity approach even remotely the figures for Däniken's books. More than thirty-seven million copies of writings from the pen of the Swiss ex-hotelkeeper have been sold to date. But what most of the grumblers I spoke of obviously didn't know was that *Erinnerungen* was not the first milestone erected by Däniken in this class of literature. He had published material on the theme of god-astronauts many years earlier. An article of his, *Hatten unsere Vorfahren Besuch aus dem Weltraum?* (*Did our Ancestors have a Visit from Space?*) was published on December 8, 1964, in the German–Canadian periodical *Der Nordwesten*. This was long before Charroux's books became available in German. In 1965 the German weekly *Neues Europa* published a series of Däniken's reports which (practically) anticipated his subsequent best seller. Typical titles: 'Do we have a Utopian past?' 'Critical considerations of UFOlogy' and 'Clairvoyance—A matter of course in the year 2000?'

All over the world the name Däniken has become as common as a trade-mark, like 'Ford' or 'Coca-Cola'. Today 'Däniken' is simply a synonym for 'Astronaut-Gods'. Doesn't that suggest the possible reason(s) for the dominance of one person among all those writing in this same field? What distinguishes Erich von Däniken from his competition? What influences have determined the steep upward curve of the sales of his books?

Publisher Erwin Barth von Wehrenalp, the man primarily responsible for Däniken's books 'capturing the imagination of the world', is one of those who believes he knows the answer. 'Of course I was familiar with a whole row of books dealing with these themes, but I had the impression that here a unique manuscript lay before me, one written by someone with an especial personal involvement. At the same time I wish to emphasise that not one of the earlier books dealing with similar themes had met with any remarkable success. One must be absolutely clear on this point: The great breakthrough in popular demand for *all* books on these theses followed on the heels of Däniken's first book.'

It was by no means easy for EvD to get a foothold in a publishing house. Even ECON was far from eager when Däniken's raw manuscript landed on a reader's desk. After a couple of weeks it was returned to the hopeful author. A few politely-turned phrases attempted to allay the sting of the final word: *Rejected*.

Däniken's friend and travelling companion Hans Neuner remembers this situation well. 'Erich didn't fool himself; he knew how difficult it was to break into the book market. To begin with, ECON had declared that they liked the manuscript, but couldn't see their way clear to publishing it.'

After that first rejection Däniken had appealed for help to Thomas von Randow, editor of the newspaper *Die Zeit*, who had passed his own recommendation on to his friend Wehrenalp. The latter relented, and the manuscript of the 'emotional non-author' (as he labelled EvD in a *Spiegel* interview) was finally set in type.

According to Wehrenalp, he *wanted* to be convinced by the 'unique' personality of von Däniken. Indeed, a publisher, willingly or not, encounters very many diverse types of writers; but Däniken's certainty and above all his persuasive power were incomparable. Perhaps even these would not have been sufficient to change Mr von Wehrenalp's mind. He admits this indirectly in giving reasons for his about-face in the case of Däniken.

'Look, I have extraordinary respect for Thomas von Randow. If he, the Science Editor of a newspaper as renowned as *Die Zeit*, says, "Here are theses which one must come to terms with," such a statement carries weight with me.'

And another decisive factor in the acceptance of Däniken's manuscript by ECON was a letter from Wernher von Braun in which he stated that indeed no one knew whether von Däniken was right, but that no one had the knowledge to say he was wrong. Wehrenalp was impressed.

'If a person like von Braun says such a thing instead of categorically declaring "That's nonsense!", then it is a publisher's duty to open a forum for public discussion of these new thoughts and theories.'

At their first meeting Däniken impressed Wehrenalp as 'a quite prepossessing author, with a charm one seldom sees nowadays'. EvD's publisher is absolutely convinced that the success of his books is closely bound to the Swiss's readiness to verify and collect evidence for his theses on the site and to personally view pertinent drawings and documents. This sets Däniken apart from most of the other authors writing on similar themes.

Hans Neuner recalls the episode, reported to him by EvD himself. 'Erich had heart palpitations when von Randow arranged an interview for him with the ECON-chief. Did Wehrenalp know about the young author's previous rejection? Would he be snubbed anew? His fears were unfounded; Wehrenalp hadn't the slightest idea that the manuscript now lying before him had already been rejected by an ECON reader. Many months later Erich couldn't resist telling his publisher the whole story. Goaded by the thought of how close he had come to missing this work, whose sales were now in the six-figure range, Wehrenalp waxed indignant over "those idiots in the reading department". But Erich was very amused.'

'Erich's great success can be attributed first and foremost to his personal aura,' stated Däniken's secretary Willi Dünnenberger. He is well-qualified to make such a statement, for he has daily opportunity to observe his employer at close quarters. 'Certainly, there are others who write along the same lines, Robert Charroux for one. But all these other authors shy away from publicity and avoid discussions with interested people. They can't express themselves aloud, they give no lectures, they don't spring to the barricades in defence of their ideas. Erich does all these things unceasingly.

'The greatest difference between Charroux and Däniken lies in the fact that Erich has been to a good ninety-five per cent of the places he names in his books. He carried out investigations and spoke with people right there on the spot, and made direct inquiries about various archaeological finds and inscriptions, and about local legends.'

Dünnenberger gives a typical example, which occurred in Peru. In the town of Ica, near Pisco Bay, lives the physician and amateur archaeologist Professor Xavier Cabrera. He has found hundreds of stones bearing extraordinary engravings, some with medical themes—one series depicts several stages of a heart transplantation—and others astronomical (an Inca looking at the heavens through a telescope). Robert Charroux visited the Peruvian scholar.

'But we learned that Charroux's visit to Cabrera lasted a mere three hours, including the time he spent photographing the stones. Using this scanty material he constructed an entire book, *L'enigme des Andes* (*Riddle of the Andes*). Däniken, however, spent three days just at the site where the stones were found. He questioned Dr Cabrera intensively, and shot many rolls of film, adding an exceptionally thorough department to his collection of reference material.'

NASA-Engineer Josef Blumrich also sees fundamental differences between the research procedures of the Swiss and those of other experts in astro-archaeology.

'From what I can gather reading books on similar themes—Charroux comes first to mind—Däniken is the only one who doesn't merely tell tall tales. He's also the only one who draws his conclusions from personal investigation: "... consequently, we must have had visits from space!" See, that's the advantage Erich has over the others.'

The NASA-expert also emphasises that in his books Däniken takes the trouble to offer suggestions for answering questions about hitherto unexplainable facts.

'He appeals to Science to apply the knowledge accumulated in the past century to archaeology as it has done, for example, in the construction of aircraft and spacecraft. I find this to be a sound, healthy and weighty argument.'

Blumrich is so completely in accord with this view that he urges it repeatedly upon listeners to his own lectures. His demand: during excavations at archaeological sites, engineers should be present.

'Indeed, archaeologists already make use of the knowledge of chemists and physicists, yet for some delvers into antiquity it is unthinkable (why, really?) to examine artifacts of earlier millennia for their possible technical origin. None of them ask themselves the question, whether five or ten thousand years ago some highly advanced culture could perhaps have flown in airships. This possibility and many others of like import are worth investigating. If the results are negative, okay—but so long as positive findings are not excluded, research should continue.'

The fact that today several branches of science pay any attention at all to 'astro-archaeology' is due principally to Erich von Däniken, the defending champion of these hypotheses. This fantastic-seeming but not totally inaccessible world of ideas—no wonder, after eight years of working together—Daniken's editor Utermann has made his own.

'First of all, thanks to Erich I'm now well-versed in the pertinent international literature,' he confessed. 'In accord with Thomas Mann's clever line, "The sceptic's advantage is that he holds everything to be possible", I now have a strong affinity for Däniken's ideas. Because everything that's said and written about him crosses my desk, I know how many stones of that mosaic are of the purest gold. Josef Blumrich's evidence that Ezekiel was probably describing a space vehicle isn't the only basis for my conviction. For when the Nobel Prizewinner and geneticist Francis H. Crick, co-author of the book *The Double Helix*, says that at some point in time an apparently extra-terrestrial inter-vention in the hereditary factors of hominids must have occurred, one does well to temper one's scepticism.'

And Crick's published statement, says Utermann, is not a unique instance; dozens of publications no longer shy away from at least admitting Däniken's theories to be in the area of the possible. 'As the intervals between such acknowledgments become ever shorter, I must admit that initially impartial, I have now become a follower, or to put it bluntly, a Däniken-fan.'

The critical comparisons made by those who know Däniken, between him and competitive writers such as Charroux, should not give rise to the impression that he fancies himself to be a cut above the others. Hans Neuner well remembers how during their travels together, EvD told of his esteem for other authors writing along similar lines. Robert Charroux was one of those discussed, and not just casually. 'On the contrary,' Neuner denied, 'Erich had great admiration for Charroux and he held the French author's books in the highest esteem.' The Tyrolean, who then began to read books on these themes at Däniken's instigation, and who now numbers himself among the initiates, believes he knows why his Swiss friend quickly attained worldwide popularity, surpassing numerous competing authors, Charroux included.

'Erich probably has more brashness, more staying-power, more perspective—and he also had the patience to bide his time until his star began to ascend. He decided early on that his present publisher was the one he wanted; to submit his work to just any publishing house was out of the question. When the subject of ECON first arose, he told me with sharp foresight—although I knew nothing of publishers or book-publishing—"Hans, if I can only crash this house, then my book has a good chance for success, because ECON is one of the top German publishers." Erich had a good nose for finding the right path.'

It wasn't only a suitable publisher that helped to launch Däniken's world-success. The Swiss's writing style contributed to his acceptance by so many readers. Theo Bos, who observed at close quarters EvD's sharp ascent from ship's steward to hotel manager to best-selling author, labels his friend's success most plausibly.

'First of all, *Erinnerungen* is uncomplicated writing. For that large segment of the population with an average education it's readily understandable, the language isn't at all difficult. The book can even be classed as recreational reading. Anyway, it's not necessary to consult reference works in order to read it. Dictionaries would be superfluous— one need not have a special education in order to be able to understand the content completely.'

Had Däniken not been unshakeably convinced of the penetrating power of his ideas, he would never have accomplished what he has, judges EvD-friend Bos. 'While he was still working on the manuscript of this first book, he was even then absolutely certain that it would be a best-seller. That certainty was the reason for the book's success!'

EvD's choice of publisher was next in contributing to the book's popularity; and finally, all the other accompanying circumstances, pleasant and unpleasant: the press-uproar and the arrest of the author. Theo Bos also judges that the first orbiting of the moon in 1968 could have been a contributing factor.

'As everyone knows, ECON held the first printing of *Erinnerungen* to a scant 6000 copies,' Bos recalls. 'They were completely sold out within two days. About a week after it appeared I tried in vain to obtain a copy—I was put on a waiting-list.'

The incredible run on Swiss bookshops by would-be readers of the first 'Däniken' was thanks to chapters published serially in the renowned Swiss weekly *Weltwoche*, which its readers devoured. The announcement that there was now an entire book available sent *Weltwoche*-readers to the booksellers in droves.

Nobody—if one excepts Däniken—least of all ECON Press itself, had reckoned on that scale of sales interest. Publisher Wehrenalp admits it openly. 'We were all surprised by the strong response. We had considered *Erinnerungen* to be sort of a contribution to discussion-groups, and we'd planned our minimal advertising accordingly. It can be shown by facts and figures: the success of the first "Däniken" was not manipulated, the book was not put over by advertising. The strong interest was clearly kindled through discussions of the theme, first in Germany, Switzerland and Austria, and then all over the world.'

Although ECON was flatly taken by surprise over the sales-boom—a salesman, as it were, who didn't believe whole-heartedly in what he was selling—the author accepted skyrocketing popular interest as a matter of course. Long before, on the day of his first visit to the sceptical publisher, Däniken had predicted the overwhelming success of *Erinnerungen*.

'Naturally, authors must be convinced of the potential success of their work,' says the ECON-boss, 'but such absolute conviction I have very seldom seen. As a matter of fact, Erich von Däniken has a sort of sixth sense in many other respects.' Even though von Wehrenalp—as he did for example during the Ecuador-fracas—now stands solidly behind his top-rank writer, it shouldn't be overlooked that he was not initially carried away by the theme his protégé championed. Indeed, this is proved by the meagre press-run of the first book.

On February 27, 1968, EvD was the happiest man in the world. Before him lay the first copy of his *Erinnerungen*. On March 1, *Weltwoche* printed the first instalment. Däniken's 'sixth sense' made a prediction: it wouldn't stick at a 6000-copy first edition. This had hardly hit the bookshops before he was already imploring the publisher to proceed with a second edition. At first, in Düsseldorf they smiled at the greenhorn's impatience, but soon the smiles disappeared. Before the month was over, the second edition had been printed and the third was under way; within one month *Erinnerungen* had reached its 20th thousand. Further editions followed, 10,000-copy runs in June and July and 25,000 in August, the doldrum-month for book sales. At the end of 1968 ECON proudly listed a total of 146,372 copies sold. In Däniken's own country a book-avalanche was turned loose; the Swiss bookshops sold 20,000 copies within eight months. 'Dänikenitis' had broken out like an epidemic.

Nine years later, there has been no lull in requests for EvD's 'first-born'. Even in Poland, where it was displayed for the first time at the 1975 Warsaw Book Fair, a first edition of 20,000 sold out in eight days. 'At the Fair and in the bazaars the Poles almost fought duels over the book,' related Wehrenalp, who had attended the Fair. To illustrate his words, *Erinnerungen* awakened an enthusiasm which—ever-larger editions notwithstanding—none of his following five books has quite managed to effect.

In Turkey 67,000 copies were disposed of in one year. In India the book appears in three languages. There are pirated editions, in Iran for instance; and although in Iceland everyone reads English, a publisher has printed Icelandic editions of all Däniken's books.

By now America has proved to be fertile soil for the Swiss's god-theories. More than 13 million copies of his books—all but the latest, *Beweise* (*Proofs*), have been published there to date—found buyers in the USA. No wonder that Wehrenalp ventures an audacious summing-up, further encouragement to the balance of success of Däniken's books: 'To me it's an established fact—the intellectual impetus given by Erich von Däniken has developed in unforeseen ways, in us his friends, and also in his adversaries. In any case it's obvious that the cerebral push his books gave and still give cannot be ignored. It's a noteworthy phenomenon, and its worldwide.'

Däniken's friend Walter Ernsting sees certain parallels between EvD and other writers. 'Erich writes a work of non-fiction with so much suspense that it reads like a novel. Here he resembles the English writer Arthur C. Clarke, author of *2001—A Space Odyssey*, who has not only written many other excellent science-fiction novels and short stories, but also non-fiction books and articles on space which are just as exciting to read as his science-fiction. I am forever comparing these two, Clarke and Däniken. Their styles and treatment are similar, and they explain their themes in the same concise manner. That's just what Däniken understood very well—that's why his first book was such a resounding success.'

Ernsting, who has been writing science fiction with world-wide success for the past two decades, seems to me to be the right person to analyse the reasons for the huge editions of Däniken's books.

'What makes Erich different from authors of the same persuasion is above all his dynamic writing style. When one takes, for example, Pauwels-Bergier's *Morning of the Magicians*, the astro-archaeological topic is in my opinion treated in a way that intimidates the reader. The book interested, even fascinated me—but I believe it doesn't have nearly the effect on the average reader that Erich's does, for his style is tight, terse and wholly absorbing.'

And that's the reason Däniken could rise to the status of most-successful author. 'Not only because of his theme,' Ernsting spelled out, '—when *Erinnerungen* appeared, this topic was no longer new, and many other authors had been writing about it for years; but their books were never able to capture the popular imagination. This situation changed as soon as Däniken appeared in the book market. Subsequently, practically all like-minded writers—including those whose works were published before EvD—profited from the world-interest in astronautical theories which Däniken had kindled.'

However, all Däniken-experts do not hold the same opinion. NASA-engineer Josef Blumrich doesn't go along with the rest; he finds Däniken's writing style atrocious.

'Actually, Erich's success is a still-unexplained phenomenon, which I suppose is partly due to the fact that his first book appeared at the best possible time. It could also be in part explainable in the context of his convincing arguments. But certainly not on the basis of his writing style. Personally, I judge the street-style in which the Däniken books are written to be frantic and unacceptable. I know a great many people who are well-inclined toward Erich but who nevertheless share my view. For them too, the style of Däniken's books is horrible.'

Utz Utermann, a trained writer of highest rank, is not exactly delighted with Blumrich's opinion. The negative attitude of the former NASA engineer is also a slap at him. It is obvious that the personal style of any editor or rewriter 'tints' his work to some extent. This in spite of taking every precaution not to influence the original author's form. When Däniken's first book appeared, the wildest rumours began circulating. Vital parts of the text had been cut and others added by the publisher. Was it also true that Utermann's hand in the shaping of Däniken's book reached beyond the usual duties of an editor? Was he EvD's 'ghostwriter'?

Utermann reacted waspishly to the suggestion. 'That's utter nonsense! As far as professional writing goes, Erich is completely self-taught. His ideas were original indeed, though for me a Book of Seven Seals; I had as yet no interest in these themes. In reading the original manuscript, however, I soon realised that he was throwing real pearls away; electrifying facts he considered taken for granted were being dispensed at less than their true value. Such pearls I only replaced in their dramatically-correct setting, an operation familiar to every writing professional.'

Utermann continued: 'Another example—Erich had overloaded his manuscript with religious-philosophical reflections, whereas I thought he already had a full measure of dynamite, enough to shake up his readers. Why should he throw on an additional burden of such controversial and difficult problems? So I eliminated or radically abridged such passages—of course, with the consent of the author.'

At first von Däniken was not too happy over this 'censorship'. Hans Neuner, who accompanied his friend on this first venture into the book-world, remembers well the tug-of-war that went on between Davos and Düsseldorf.

'Utermann's rewriting style didn't deviate very much from the original except for his choice of words. Erich had said it short and sweet, expressed many ideas in an entirely natural and uncomplicated way. Then here came Utermann, who curtailed much or simply crossed it out. And who gave as reason for his rewriting the need to "polish" Däniken's text. *That* is simply not to be used, or *this* he could not be responsible for. Another thing he said was that it was too crudely formulated.'

Anyway, EvD didn't let himself become discouraged. In a letter he wrote me on January 14, 1969 (he was in remand detention in Vienna at the time) he wrote astutely: 'I had originally included many Bible passages in *Erinnerungen*, but the publisher found my inferences too daring and cut them down to the few which remain. But in my next book (title: *Return to the Stars*) I'll put them all back in together with some unrestrained scoffing, and between the lines a little dynamite.'

Utermann laughed when he heard of Däniken's defiant reaction. 'You mustn't forget how *Erinnerungen* came about. At the time he wrote it Däniken had the lease of the Davos Hotel Rosenhügel hanging around his neck. He had worries—money was short. There wasn't much spare time to work continuously on his manuscript. He wrote during an hour or two snatched here and there, mostly at night, as I know now. Isn't it logical to assume that if one is subjected to such stress, repetitions will creep into one's writing? Sometimes weeks or even months intervened between passages he wrote down. So Erich would think, when he sat once more at his writing-desk, "I must say such-and-such to my readers," forgetting completely that earlier he had said the exact same thing in other words. Part of my job was to remove such undesired repetition.'

Today the situation is entirely different, says Utermann, who has long ago gained Däniken's trust, and resigned from his position as 'censor'. 'Nothing like that will happen to Erich again. By now he is able to write his books undisturbed, in one sweep from beginning to end.'

But what EvD subsequently accepted—namely, allowing his manuscript to be professionally edited—was offensive to Blumrich from the very beginning. ECON Press had considered letting his first book, *Da tat sich der Himmel auf* (*The Spaceships of Ezekiel*), be rewritten. Not because it was badly written; on the contrary, to make the technical, rather dry text more readable. Wehrenalp therefore handed the manuscript over to his trained editor Utermann. He had reworked scarcely half of the manuscript when Blumrich got wind of it. His raging protest brought the rewriting to a halt. He violently rejected any attempt to 'dress up' his work, and didn't wish his book to be (re-) written in the style found in popular periodicals.

So it happens that Blumrich's book about the prophet Ezekiel—as far as style goes—is sort of a hybrid, half bearing Utermann's stamp, half Blumrich's. It must be emphasised, however, that the NASA-engineer's aversion to the style in which Däniken's books are written is entirely apart from his personal relationship with EvD and Utermann; they are good friends all around.

Theo Bos believes that he has discovered an underestimated strength of the god-seeker in contrast to his writing competition. 'Erich differs from other writers in that his books do not forget *humour*. His chapters aren't—as are many of the others'—composed with animal-like intensity. He doesn't immerse himself unduly in scholarly waffle. More important to him is the questioning, the wondering, the "is it possible?" or "would it be conceivable?" Compare him with the Frenchmen Pauwels, Bergier or Charroux. They remain objective and dry, they're boring to read. True, they present facts, but they're on guard against too-provocative thought-patterns. In the end, Erich's popularity is based on just this deliberate provocation. Posing these questions to be argued over, let the chips fall where they may—I see that as Däniken's great plus, as his advantage over his competition.'

Humour as a foundation for worldwide success? Why not? Stuttgart Professor of Geology Hans Georg Wunderlich, author of several popular books on scientific topics, holds a similar opinion. It might be fascinating to read Wunderlich's views about the reasons for Däniken's success. They came out under pressure from the professor's 'dear colleagues'. In his book *Wohin der Stier Europa trug* (*The Secret of Crete*) Wunderlich complains about the scorn of those envious ones who decried the geologist's departure from scientific orthodoxy in his studies of the Minoan culture, some saying, 'We have a Däniken among us!'

Possibly the self-defence of the embattled scholar consisted—following the maxim 'attack is the best defence'—of keeping clear of the stigma of a 'Däniken-image'. On the other hand, what resulted was a somewhat schizoid attitude on the part of Wunderlich; he can't help indicating a certain admiration for the successful career of the best-selling Swiss author. We read in *The Secret of Crete:*

> My secret hope that Erich von Däniken will some day let his cat out of the bag is probably doomed to disappointment. But at the risk of betraying Däniken's secret strategy and spoiling his joke, I venture to assert that he is the most important and most brilliant satirist in German literature for at least a century. It really doesn't matter what this subtle intellect writes about cosmic visitors who have set up, for their own amusement, a global terrarium on earth with experimentally 'enriched' apes. Däniken's wit is implicit not in the exact shape of his fantasies but in his biting satire of an influential school of scientific thinking. This master literary spoofer and creator of a new genre of cosmicomic books is merely carrying to the extreme a method that has been pursued by eminent archaeologists, and that even Arthur Evans was guilty of. At the turn of the century bathrooms and flush toilets were among the symbols of modern progress. In old Berlin the bathtub from the Hotel Adlon used to be carried to the Royal Palace whenever His Majesty wished to take a bath. Evans promptly found bathtubs and toilets in his excavations. A short while ago a fad for home grills swept West Germany. Sure enough, grills were soon found in the Büdelsdorf excavations of a Neolithic site. Today space travel is the *dernier cri* of civilization; therefore Däniken finds evidence for it in the excavation sites of cultures going back to the Stone Age. A glorious jest!

Erich von Däniken, accosted about this singular analysis by an interviewer from the American magazine *Playboy* and questioned about the truth of the assertions, didn't let the chance for publicity (showman of his times) escape him. Why should he deny what people who can hear the grass grow want to discover within his secret self? So he retorted poker-faced:

> The answer is yes and no. We have a wonderful word for it in German: *jein*. In many respects I am absolutely no satirist; I earnestly mean what I say. On the other hand, I like to make people laugh.

Does he really mean that?

CHAPTER VII

Däniken's 'Young Men'

Literary 'counter-evidence', fabricated for the purpose of checking Däniken's book-avalanche and shaking the credibility of the author, was produced but to no avail. The competition was perturbed; heavier weapons must be brought to bear. And so it came to pass that the spotlight was turned on EvD's private life. A malevolent intrusion into Däniken's intimate sphere. Every wisp of hearsay which could be used against him was uttered during Däniken's trial, which opened in 1970 in Chur, Switzerland.

A swell of rumours was released through a 'psychiatric expert', Dr Erich Weber of the Beverin Clinic, who had been commisioned by the District Attorney's Office. With sham reluctance he offered an 'expert opinion' of the accused Erich von Däniken which boiled down to a general condemnation. *Der Spiegel* reporter Gerhard Mauz, well-versed in courtroom procedure, asked uneasily:

> What do these laws allow? they permit the psychiatrist, engaged on behalf of the Examining Magistrate, to act not as an independent authority but rather as a subordinate of the District Attorney's Office. The questions on which the psychiatrist had to express himself were set for him by the Examining Magistrate and the District Attorney. When the psychiatrist worked out his Expert Opinion he based it on the established guilt of the defendant—which only the verdict should find to be correct or incorrect.

One could put this resumé in plainer words: What was done in Chur was a prearranged affair. As publisher von Wehrenalp commented, 'As to the Expert Opinion of Dr Weber, I can only ask, "Who gives an Expert Opinion on such a psychiatrist?" '

Before the court Dr Weber dealt with the accused even more severely than in his written opinion. He didn't limit himself to testimony on

86

what had been requested of him, which should have been his duty; no, the upright and eminent gentleman played to the spectators 'as if he was the artist Hodler painting a wall-mural' (Mauz), with the definite aim of demolishing Däniken's image as a successful author. Indeed he also undertook—beneath the shelter of his 'Expert Opinion'—to make excursions into sexual and literary fields, and took pleasure in occupying himself with Däniken's family history, so that his *evidence* led to 'the indictment proving to be true' (Dr Weber).

He had felt an 'inner opposition to the wild fancies of the accused', admitted the lean psychiatrist with the Jesuit-profile (Mauz) with loathing; additionally, both of Däniken's books (only two were then in print) presented hypotheses in journalistic fashion, as if they were facts. He wrote about genetics without being a geneticist—such books could elicit from serious scientists only a pitying smile.

But pity was foreign to Dr Weber's nature. He believed he was able to plumb the inscrutable wickedness of Däniken from an enthusiastic letter which EvD had written to his friend Hans Neuner.

This amateur Sherlock Holmes had deduced that the accused must have homo- or bi-sexual tendencies or else a weak libido, which Weber attributed to a testicular operation Däniken had undergone in his youth. In any case, the accused was able to have 'only a superficial relationship to his wife and child'.

After issuing this pronouncement, the respectable expert of course had to admit that his insinuations had no bearing on the trial proceedings nor any connection with the indictment. A heavy heart accompanied his 'Expert Opinion', he stated with hypocritical compassion. *Spiegel* reporter Gerhard Mauz was apparently 'moved' and wrote ironically: 'One sees the burden he bears, and is glad for him when after discussing in detail whether homo or bi, he remembers that sexual frailties have no significance in this case.'

But why had psychiatrist Weber nevertheless washed Däniken's 'dirty linen' in public? Was it his intention—and on whose orders?—to influence the jury's verdict? We don't want to digress; the trial and the 'offences' charged to Erich von Däniken are covered in an addendum to the book. *Here* we're dealing with the no less spectacular accusation as to whether EvD is homo- or bi-sexual. Significantly—aside from the public accusation of the respectable Dr Weber—such rumours are usually spread in a whispering campaign. To publicise that sort of nonsense in a newspaper is too risky; the mildest consequence would have been a counterblast from other news organs.

However that may be, such rumours really do circulate, and potential opponents of various stripes attempt to keep them alive. Aside from the fact that homosexuality (where minors are not involved) has long been exempt from penalty in progressive countries, the sexual impulse is an individual's private affair—nobody's business but his own. But in EvD's case, what are the facts about this unsubstantiated rumour? Indeed it's well known that if one scatters false charges about long enough they'll eventually strike a spark, and one's primary objective is attained. Some black speck remains forever on the otherwise white waistcoat. Even psychiatrist Dr Weber chose this method, protected by the (pseudo-)scientific cloak of his profession. Defamation campaigns may be waged in many ways.

Theo Bos, Däniken-expert from the old days, is in the know on this point of information. During their work together in Davos EvD and the Hollander had to share one room for reasons of economy. 'There was only one bed in the room, a French double-bed. So what else could we do but sleep in it? Today I can say without false shame, "I once slept with the famous Erich von Däniken." But homosexual—no, that he is positively not. If it were true I surely would have known it.'

But Theo Bos knows what fed such rumours and is in a position to refute them. 'If one accepts as a reason for believing Erich is homosexual the fact that he takes young men along with him on his travels, then the suspicion arises that the belief was snatched from thin air, and has to do with envy.'

Bos knows his Däniken, and he also knows what troubles lie in ambush on expeditions such as EvD undertakes. For him it's neither chance nor libidinous intention that EvD places implicit value on travelling with young companions.

'Let's suppose for a moment that Erich tried travelling with an older person or one his own age. A fan of his if possible. Clearly, the other would be enthusiastic. So many new impressions would burst upon him. Cities he'd never seen, museums containing artifacts unknown to him till then. The fan would be beside himself, exuberant. He would be constantly assailing his chief with "Look there, Mr von Däniken, what can that be?" and "This is surely a such-and-such!" That's the way such a tour would go. In his enthusiasm a fan would try, with of course the best of intentions, to drag Erich into his own field of interest. Erich wouldn't like that at all. On his research trips he's concentrated upon and occupied with the purpose of the journey: to track down evidence to back up his theories. This can be quite strenuous, and any distraction is a hindrance.

'Not that he doesn't occasionally have discussions with other people. But when he does, it's about *his* interests and ideas. Should he let his companion inveigle him into a brief conversation on some other subject, it might possibly last for days. Time literally *stolen* from Däniken the researcher.'

Even though he himself has never gone along on an expedition, Bos knows from his friends' reports exactly what occurs on such a trip, and that trials and tribulations are always considerable.

'If Erich travels with a younger person, it's for the reason that he can depend on his companion's endurance. I believe that on these almost always strenuous trips an older person would simply become exhausted after the first week or two. Enthusiasm exists mainly before the trip starts. Not that Erich lets the impending exertions go unmentioned, though one knows what they are indeed. Who admits in advance that perhaps it might finally be too much for him? Therefore one feigns vigour and stamina, verbally disposes of all the pre-announced difficulties, says, "Of course, Mr von Däniken, I'll carry the trunk. Naturally, I'll ride the donkey with you. Sure, I'll push the jeep. *I* have no fear of snakes, I even like spiders. Tropical diseases don't scare me. No, no, Mr von Däniken, believe me, none of that makes any difference!"

'After two or three weeks of genuine torture, disillusionment arrives. "Oh God, another donkey ride. Why is the jeep always breaking down? What—there are snakes here too!? I loathe spiders, the nauseating creatures! I feel miserable, have I caught some germ again? Always on the go—can't I sleep undisturbed for 24 hours just one time?" And so it goes, a lament with many nerve-deadening verses. Now you see why Erich always travels with young companions. They simply have —Erich picks them very carefully—more involvement in his projects. They know what Däniken plans and strives for and they're not forever asking, "Why are we doing this? Why not that?"

'And something else: A younger companion feels himself to be— even though it may not so appear—an employee of Däniken's; after all, he's being paid a salary. An older person is more sensitive in such matters. He's no longer a lad, and shouldn't have to take orders from a Däniken who's his same age or perhaps even younger than he is. These are fundamental barriers. Erich makes a clear distinction: here is friendship, there is employer-employee relationship. Older persons don't always realise that.'

The fact that Erich von Däniken never travels with women is based on similar reasons, and certainly cannot be attributed to his non-existent homosexual preferences. Mrs von Däniken must know. 'Earlier,' she said, 'I would have been happy to go along with my husband, but couldn't because of Cornelia, who was then too small. Today I'm glad that I don't have to go, for these research trips are in part very primitive and difficult, and Erich's lecture tours rather strenuous.'

Däniken's spouse presents reasonable arguments. One notes that she speaks from the experience of over one-and-one-half decades of married life. She understands how she fits into the present situation. 'It's like this—when one knows a partner as long as I've known my husband, occasional disagreements cannot be avoided. Then should we travel together, exhaustion sets in after about eight days at the most. One starts to get venomous. Were your travelling companion a stranger, you'd make a desperate effort to get along—but with your spouse you'd probably let yourself fly off the handle. That's another reason why today I see no real advantage in accompanying Erich on his trips.'

Although the world-traveller's wife doesn't maintain a grand mansion, it's large enough to keep her going around the clock. In addition she has two dogs to care for, the Saint Bernard Neptun, and Luna, the Highland Terrier, his diminutive opposite. Besides, there's the Dänikens' pride, a medium-sized, neatly-kept orchard on a slope near the house, which likewise needs taking care of. Still another reason why Elisabeth von Däniken does not want to embark on exhausting journeys with her husband.

But it is neither the house and garden nor the dogs that have really led to this decision. Mrs von Däniken thinks first and foremost of her daughter Cornelia. Although the 14-year-old girl is quite self-reliant, her mother wants to avoid any eventuality which could rob the child of both of her parents. Däniken's voyages of discovery in the domains of his gods are made almost exclusively by air, and his wife feels this is not entirely without danger.

'So if sometime something happens, there should always be one parent to take care of Lela,' says Mrs von Daniken. She is learning English, just to keep up with her daughter and also, as she says, 'to keep intellectually fit'.

Inspected from these angles it's understandable why Erich von Däniken sees no point in travelling with women. But does that signify that he's homosexually oriented? When he is accosted on this topic, his temperature rises.

'Well—God Almighty, once again—should I, a happily-married man, go travelling with a feminine companion? Isn't it evident to any average citizen that with such a person, who would necessarily be young and attractive (otherwise she wouldn't be working for me), sexual contact would be unavoidable? And then the domestic quarrels, and the divorce with all that it entails. The talkative tale-tellers themselves—those who are married—ought to try travelling with young women for a few weeks. Then they'd know what would undoubtedly happen.

'Should I travel with girls, so that every day and every night there'd be a love scene? No one could expect me to be such an imbecile!'

Secretary Willi Dünnenberger knows from his own observations: 'Erich loves being straightforward. If he likes someone he says so. If he says "I like you" it has absolutely nothing to do with homosexuality. This holds good even when one knows that on their travels Erich and his companion sleep in the same room. The reason for that is because Erich doesn't like being alone while abroad. It isn't in his nature when the day's work is done, to part company at the other's hotel room door saying "Ciao, see you in the morning!" Whoever accompanies Erich is also a friend, and after an eventful day—with Erich almost every day is eventful—they have a drink together in their room, discuss the day's happenings and finally fall into a more refreshing sleep than if they'd just gone off to bed alone. Erich wouldn't like that at all.'

And still one more reason why EvD prefers to travel with youthful companions: 'A 40- or 50-year-old person on such trips couldn't take a subordinate role as readily as a 20-year-old. For Erich is always the boss. An agreeable one, I must admit. But would a fifty-year-old man submit to Däniken's commands on every occasion? Would he obey Erich's orders, "Come on, do this!"—"Look sharp, do that!" with no back-talk?' Here Dünnenberger and Bos are of the same mind.

Today Hans Neuner is still irritated over the psychiatric evaluation of EvD made during his trial.

'I simply can't explain it to myself—how such a renowned psychiatrist as Dr Weber could express such a one-sided opinion. When he, as an expert, must know better how to form an estimate of a person's strengths and weaknesses.' He's especially indignant over Weber's publicly-voiced suspicion that Erich is homo- or bi-sexual. A slur that had nothing to do with the offences with which he was charged.

'Certainly, every person has a tendency to bi-sexuality,' says Neuner, dealing dispassionately with this controversial topic. 'The situation comes up occasionally, perhaps in prison, in the front lines or during hours of utter loneliness—hence in distress. Do you believe that it upsets anyone, if a man thus ill-used by fate yields to homosexual tendencies? He finds himself in an extraordinary situation, is a slave to his drives, as it were. However, that's not to say he'd act the same way in his everyday life. There he has everything he needs: his recreations, his diversions, his normal sexual activity. . . .'

And, concerning Erich von Däniken, 'It's therefore special circumstances that influence a person's behaviour. Only this parallel—and I speak from my own experience—doesn't hold true in Erich's case. I've travelled with him throughout the world long enough, and I can't imagine how he could have held himself back all this time if he really had homosexual intentions. This very same Erich, who is in the habit of heading straight towards his goal. . . .'

This delicate subject was in no way 'taboo' for Däniken and Neuner. Frequently, said the Tyrolean, 'but only incidentally, when once again such a rumour reached our ears,' were these problems discussed.

'Erich had candidly confessed (if one can say "confessed") that he knew very well what various people thought about him, that they took him to be a homosexual. We had profound discussions on the subject, openly voicing our respective views and opinions. Erich didn't leave me in the dark, saying that as a man he'd found relatively little connection with the feminine world. In my opinion he saw such minimal contact as more intellectual than sexual.

'For that reason I don't believe he could be homosexual, because he cultivates none of his relationships on a sexual basis. He simply doesn't require it.'

In his time Theo Bos also discussed emotional problems with Däniken. Sensitive subjects including love, friendship and marriage were touched upon. Even homosexuality, although only superficially.

'For instance, we spoke about the correspondence between Richard Wagner and his friend Mathilde Wesendonck—correspondence which first became public some time after Wagner's death. These letters spoke about love, about friendship between man and woman, friendship between woman and woman and that between man and man.' Bos began to philosophise—remembrances of things past.

'Friendship between man and woman—that's wedlock, is love. Friendship from woman to woman is sometimes only contrived, unfortunately. Friendships between women almost always bear a stamp of mistrust. Each wants to know everything about the other: Why do you do it like that? Why not this way? And even when they compliment each other, it's unquestionably not on the basis of their conduct.

'It's otherwise with friendships, genuine friendships between two men. One tells the other what's happened, his friend takes it all in but asks no questions. He knows what's what, and that's enough for him; he understands his partner's behaviour. That's the way the friendship between Erich and me operates. When he says something to me, I accept it without question. If Erich tells me about somebody or other, I listen. He does the same; he doesn't question me, but he gives advice if I ask for it. This from deep-seated empathy.'

Are such motivations impure? Does friendship between men go hand in hand with abnormality, with aberration? Such suspicions are complete nonsense. Unfortunately, and groundlessly, they are often voiced. I too have not been spared this vilification. The instigators of the unhappy incident were journalists from the Catholic encampment. Däniken and I were speaking at a meeting in the charming resort city of Baden, near Vienna. An enterprising Baden bookseller, August Breininger, had arranged our co-presentation, to be held in the city's Savings-Bank meeting room, which seated 250 comfortably.

But on this day, August 22, 1974, the word 'comfort' didn't apply. The lecture-hall threatened to burst at the seams. More than 400 Däniken-hungry spectators were packed like sardines into the hot, stuffy room. Another 200 who couldn't gain entry (the police had finally blocked further access) pressed their noses against the hall's entrance doors. What they missed optically was at least offered acoustically; Mr Breininger had mounted loudspeakers outside the bank. The square in front of the building was overflowing with listeners.

I opened the meeting, reading from my book *Gott kam von den Sternen*, which had appeared shortly before. Then Däniken gave a lecture with accompanying slides. It was a fascinating presentation, and when it was over EvD and I missed by a hair being sacrificed to the besieging autograph-seekers.

A successful guest-appearance—so we thought in our naïveté. We were set straight two weeks later. A journalist from the Catholic weekly *Neue Bildpost*—he had contented himself with a pre-lecture interview with Däniken, and was not present at the meeting—had written a report on the event. In his own fashion, throwing in everything possible—except the truth.

Consequently, readers of the *Bildpost* learned about the brawls at the bank entrance which smashed the glass doors; they read about a Däni-ken who had departed indignantly from the 'inhospitable town', and they read an assortment of invented assertions and malicious insinu-ations. A 'report' replete with falsehoods.

To crown their turpitude the Christian news sheet, oozing humane-ness, said (*Neue Bildpost*, Nr. 38/1974): '... in the next two years Däniken indicated he would seldom be around. He intends to set out for the Middle East with a Land Rover and one or two of his young men—*a circumstance which has already led to overt reproofs* ...' [italics mine].

These lines, evidently intended to impute abnormal acts to EvD, didn't require more detailed explanation. EvD and I demanded an immediate rectification, failing which we threatened court action. I felt that this insinuation was also addressed to me, as a few lines before those quoted I had been labelled as one of Däniken's 'young men'.

The *Bildpost* people began to sweat. Two editions later a retraction appeared. In a separate box the editor added an apology, and admitted that the wording of the original report was inaccurate. A trial would have been quite disagreeable for the pseudo-Christian gentlemen.

One who would have been the first to know if all this homosexual rumour-mongering about Erich were true is his older brother Otto. I spoke to him openly about it, and his opinion was plain and precise.

'This absurd idea originated, as did other absurdities, with that head-shrinker, the psychiatrist Dr Weber. I know my brother very well indeed; I've discussed profundities with him through many an alcohol-fogged night. So I know how Erich thinks about these things. For him sex is a windfall of delight, a stroke of good fortune. It's what one calls love, and something more than that. To his imputed homosexuality I say "Nonsense!"'

'Admittedly, I'm uninformed about Erich's correspondence with male friends and associates; I know no details of letters he's exchanged with his travelling companions. But I do know all his youthful friends from the time when he was a steward-apprentice; I was around then quite often. If one of Erich's friends was ill at home or in hospital, my brother would bring him flowers and candy, and write pages-long letters of comfort.

'It's correct—Erich has a different relationship with men than he has with women. But don't we all? Do you, Mr Krassa, deal with your female friends in the same manner as with your male ones?'

According to Otto von Däniken, psychiatrist Weber couldn't seem to swallow the fact that the numerous (male) friends of his brother—in spite of strong accusations by various news organs—still kept their loyalty to him and wrote him encouraging letters. And that for his part this prisoner, while under constant stress, wrote amiable, even consoling messages in return. The narrow-minded head-doctor deformed the meaning of this rapport to fit his 'Expert Opinion'.

With my provocatively-posed questions before him, Otto von Däniken made a direct spot-check. He took up the telephone, dialled a certain number, and his brother Erich was on the line. The short dialogue speaks for itself.

OTTO: Tell me, Erich, how would you react today if somebody labelled you 'gay'?

ERICH: That would depend on *who* said it. I'd give an intellectual demagogue his own answer, using *his* weapons. I'd ask a foolish person, 'Why, are you one?' And a journalist would probably hear, 'Would it disturb you? Are you against it?'

A normally-educated and informed person would never ask me your question!

95

CHAPTER VIII

A Verbal Execution

Five pm on Friday, February 13, 1970—and a very unlucky day for Erich von Däniken. In the sparsely-occupied high council chamber of the Graubünden courthouse in Chur, one of the most spectacular trials in recent Swiss history is coming to an end. Presiding Judge Rolf Raschein pronounces sentence. The accused Erich von Däniken is found guilty of repeated and continued embezzlement, continued and professional fraud and repeated and continued forging of documents.

Raschein dictates the penalty; it is severe: three and a half years in prison, less 300 days remand detention already served, 3000 francs fine, and suspension of civil rights for two years after sentence is served.

Erich von Däniken subsequently suffered a nervous breakdown. Until the sentence was read the ex-hotelier from Davos hadn't given up hope: hope for a spark of justice, a spark of sympathy.

> Heavenly justice is not meant here, not the natural justice of human conscience, but rather the bloodless justice which expunged that line from the Lord's Prayer: ... and forgive us our debts as we forgive our debtors. ...

These words of Gottfried Keller's were quoted by *Spiegel* reporter Gerhard Mauz at the beginning of his account of the course of the trial. A long-time observer of courtrooms, and unbiased for or against Erich von Däniken, Mauz reflected:

> There are verdicts which tell more about the judge than about the judged. The Graubünden court succumbed to the temptation to examine not only the business manipulations of Erich von Däniken but also the success of the writer Erich von Däniken. For these contemporaries who read the author von Däniken, the swindler von

Däniken was an affront to their dignity. The court wanted to strike the accused Däniken with Däniken's success, and with the same blow the world, which allowed such success to occur.

Gerhard Mauz also took Däniken's sympathisers to task, reproving them—with some justification—for holding a superficial attitude towards Swiss justice.

... when von Däniken, at the instigation of the Graubünden District Attorney, was arrested in Vienna on November 19, 1968, his friends were immediately at hand. One should be fearful of such friends; from then until Däniken's transfer to Chur in February 1969, they unleashed a publicity campaign that arose ostensibly from the troubles of the best-seller author.

Instead of arguing with Swiss criminal procedure—an opportunity offered by the Däniken case—the so-called Friends of Swiss Justice, particularly those from Graubünden Canton, launched a personal attack: 'This is official despotism.' Where the position of the Swiss District Attorney's Office should have been discussed, they took blind issue with the District Attorney personally. They didn't concern themselves with the basic questions centering on an occasional von Däniken case, but rather tried to gain ground by shouting a general mistrust of the administration of the law.

Coloured by an uneasiness derived from experience with Justice's unequally-weighted scales, the *Spiegel* court expert's reactions were not wholly dispassionate. Friends and 'friends' are two different things. The pro-Däniken journalists were inspired to give qualified support to a man who had been treated unjustly, who, incidentally, had written a best seller. Much more, it was the need for something sensational to give the reading public, a need which several popular journalists were only too willing to fill. But Gerhard Mauz—the man who tried to be balanced and objective about this 'case'—knew the imprisoned Swiss and his friends barely or not at all. As a result, he lumped them all together. He dismissed a miscellany of differing opinions and actions in one fell swoop.

After the Graubünden District Attorney's Office had answered the press campaign against it with the surprising disclosure of previous offences by Däniken, 'and in addition—not without cunning—introduced the psychiatric evaluation of Däniken ... hastily transforming Paul back into Saul' (Mauz), it was soon evident which way the wind blew.

Walter Ernsting: 'When Erich was arrested in Vienna in November of 1968, I was firmly convinced that certain institutions were behind the event, that the whole thing was contrived to break him. Today I am more of the opinion that it was a coup engineered by one man, a man who hated Däniken. A simple act of vengeance.' The science-fiction writer's opinion is that it isn't really so difficult, by using some current law or other, to put a man behind bars.

'Any man who walks on muddy roads ends up with mud on his shoes. I'd like to see the person who would dare to say without blushing, "Not me!" So, it wasn't especially difficult to nail the rather reckless Däniken. Anyway, today I *am* sure that the Examining Magistrate simply handled this case as he did because of an inferiority complex. He couldn't bear it that Däniken, whom he knew, was successful, while he himself had no opportunity to rival that success. For him it was a way of satisfying his feelings of envy, to see the man whom he hated arrested and imprisoned.'

Who is this man, who with grim determination and on his own initiative, ordered Erich von Däniken's arrest? Who—as Theo Bos suspects with good reason—through a spectacular trial wanted to use Däniken to further his own career?

Rocholl and Roggersdorf have investigated this question; they spoke with attorneys, recorded their statements on tape, and using these tapes and other data from Swiss political figures, assembled a portrait of this other 'Anti-Däniker'. So who is Hans-Peter Kirchhofer, Examining Magistrate in the Graubünden District Attorney's office? How can we describe him?

From an extensive assortment of opinions about him quoted in *Das seltsame Leben des Erich von Däniken* I made a random selection. They derive from various people whose names do not matter. But the mosaic of observations presents a strikingly accurate and thorough characterisation of this Swiss jurist in the service of Graubunden Canton.

> ... Kirchhofer is probably very ambitious, and he's extremely conceited ... Kirchhofer is of average height, but appears taller because he's quite corpulent, indeed fat ... He appears inflated. I've heard that colleagues call him a 'puffed-up frog' ... I heard that he once complained that he'd made no friends at all in Davos. Readily conceivable—it must be very difficult for him to make contact with people ... Perhaps it's significant to his findings that he's unfit for the Armed Services, a shortcoming in a Swiss citizen, who is

expected to perform his reserve duty and ascend the ladder of military grades ... He runs around constantly, summers and winters, in a leather coat, actually one like staff officers wear ... Whoever opposes Kirchhofer, whether he's right or wrong, injures his vanity ... Kirchhofer is the same type as a student or scholar whose thinking is in accord with the old Code of Honour ... He has a peculiar way of holding his head, sliding the back of it down into his collar so that his nose is in the air ... He has a certain standard, one must grant him that. But his thinking is channelled into pure straight lines ... I have a very bad impression of this man ... Mr Kirchhofer made a miserable impression indeed. I wrote him from Rheinfelden about whether I could speak with Däniken, and that I'd phone as soon as I arrived in Chur. I did so, and spoke to District Attorney Padrutt, who was kind and decent, calm and objective—while the other [Kirchhofer] immediately flew into a rage and threatened me with legal action, which I really would accept with pleasure ... In Chur I wasn't granted access—they didn't allow me to see von Däniken ..

A stroll through the garden of opinions about Hans-Peter Kirchhofer clarifies many things and allows us to draw certain conclusions. It can be stated without hesitation that the Confederation's Magistrate was prejudiced. He had decided on the line he was going to take and he followed it obstinately and undeviatingly. EvD, in a letter of April 2, 1970, quoted from *Das seltsame Leben*:

Directly after the first hearing, which was conducted by Mr Kirchhofer, I had to establish that it was not managed correctly and that vital statements had been swept under the rug. When approached about this, Kirchhofer responded that he would decide what was essential, and that we would return later to the contested points. On the basis of this statement I signed the deposition.

During the following weeks depositions of witnesses were frequently read aloud to me in which important details did not conform with fact. But they made me realise that the witnesses had not been asked important questions about the accusations nor about my person. In addition it was clear to me—for I'd known some of these witnesses for years—that certain idioms and ways of speaking could not have come from those questioned.

Time and again I entered objections against the picture being painted by these documents, which—on Kirchhofer's bare say-so—were rejected as 'unfounded' ... After I'd seen that there was no chance to inject any truth in the documents, I resigned myself to my fate in the hope that by so doing, the investigation would come to an end as quickly as possible. My intention was, through questions put to the witnesses in open court, to disclose the untenable method of Kirchhofer's deposition-taking. That's why I demanded that all consenting witnesses appear before the court.

Indeed, Däniken's motion was not formally rejected, but was answered by Kirchhofer in characteristically overbearing fashion: 'As I've already said, I'm not ready to debate the subject with you!'

Erich's proposal was valid, and would have also had legal validity during the trial. The fact is, however, that the court rejected all of the witnesses for the defence. Barrister Adolf Hörler, Däniken's defence lawyer, on this point (quoted from *Das seltsame Leben*):

Our criminal trial procedure is defined by the Canton. This procedure is just ten years old (Hörler's comments were made on April 24, 1970), but it manifests the spirit of the Middle Ages: it is still very strongly influenced by the odium of the Inquisition. It starts with the investigating authority placing a boulder in the path of objectivity; then at a later time, namely during the trial, the very same officials have now become the prosecuting authority. But the question can not be examined, whether the authority in its earlier capacity was or was not objective. I myself was an Examining Magistrate for almost ten years, but I don't believe any case ever came before me where there wasn't at least one aspect in favour of the accused party!

In Däniken's 'black' case—as far as the Chur legal jurisdiction was concerned—there wasn't one white speck! Legal procedure in Graubünden Canton bears the stamp of the Middle Ages. There were no advantages for the defence lawyer Hörler; here barristers have no opportunity to examine documents in the case *before* the investigation, only after the investigation is concluded. But then how can one be certain that the indictment couldn't have been 'manipulated' in some way?

The Court reacted with typical sensitivity when the accused EvD diverted the auditorium with the *bon mot*: 'The man who tells me he never lies, lies!'

District Attorney Willy Padrutt, angrily: 'Everyone here is obviously lying. The Examining Magistrate lies. The Prosecutor lies. The witnesses lie and the judges lie!'

Däniken: Never have I said, neither before nor during these proceedings, that everyone lies, as you try to make it seem. The witnesses don't lie, the judges don't lie. And I also concede that you don't lie. But everything that you know, everything on which you build your case, originates with Mr Kirchhofer. You have not listened to me for a second during this year's imprisonment, nor have you been present while a witness gave a deposition.

Padrutt: That is also not my task.

Däniken: Then how will you know what is true?

Padrutt: From the documents!

Däniken: That's it exactly!

EvD ran in circles; all of Chur officialdom is linked together. The accused and his lawyer stood apart, completely at a loss. Everything was going against them.

Otto von Däniken: 'You ask about wire-pullers. The real wire-puller is called Kirchhofer. After Erich's arrest he was taken aback by the violent press-reaction. So he had to devise further misdemeanours to give him leverage against the publicity. It should of course be made to appear as though the misdemeanours existed *before* the arrest. An operation, by the way, which Erich reproached him for repeatedly.'

At the time of his Vienna arrest Erich was loaded with a not inconsiderable burden of debt amounting to about 400,000 francs. He had scraped the money together with the aid of various loan-sources, both banks and private patrons. The fact which led to his prosecution was that none of the lenders knew about the others. Däniken had put the 'piastres' into his money-losing Hotel Rosenhügel as well as into his travel planning, and in the course of time had become an expert in putting off his creditors. But as the 400,000 francs were not the cause of his arrest, *why* then? None of his creditors had given in to the temptation to lodge a complaint against the Davos hotel-lessee, not even when Examining Magistrate Kirchhofer had pressed them to do so. Only the Davos Resort Association gave in. As of September 1968 —EvD was on a journey at the time—they were owed almost ninety thousand francs in resort taxes, only 6000 of which were due from Däniken. Kirchhofer saw an official offence therein. He picked out this overdue amount (the other delinquent hoteliers were left unmolested) and made sure that an order for Däniken's arrest was recorded in the Swiss police report. The behaviour of the spa-association officials was strange too—before his departure EvD had agreed with these gentlemen to pay the arrears in instalments and he had been doing up to his arrest.

When the trial began, Erich von Däniken was completely out of debt. Every creditor's money had been returned, late, it's true, but in some cases with as much as eighteen per cent interest.

Brother Otto: 'Erich was racing against time then. In this affair my opinion hasn't changed; the arrest was wholly superfluous and one hundred per cent unjustified. Now at the time of the arrest I myself didn't know precisely what was really going on. But one thing we family members knew without doubt—Erich was no swindler. The criminal activities Erich was supposed to be carrying on just never existed. In my opinion they were an invention of the authorities, and their legally-valid sentence was based on that invention. Applying the same method used to label my brother as a swindler, I could put every businessman and probably half the upright Swiss citizens in the dock!'

Hans Neuner, who had been with EvD on the occasion of his arrival and arrest at Vienna's Schwechat Airport in 1968, had no idea of Däniken's financial difficulties. In his naiveté (as he admits today) he took the ready availability of funds for granted; after all, Erich was an hotelier. Däniken never burdened his travelling companion with his own money worries. 'But perhaps,' suspects Neuner, 'he didn't want to drive himself crazy over them.' At that time EvD's thoughts centered exclusively about one thing: his first book must be successful. Should this happen, his problems would clear up by themselves.

Utermann recognises deeper motives for the legal campaign against Däniken. 'Erich was the victim of a Davos cabal. It started out with simple unspoken bias against him. Not officially of course—but if you only knew the clannish spirit within some Swiss Cantons!

'What Erich presumed to do in his capacity as hotelier was suspect to the Davos business community. 1. He received peculiar guests such as Professor Oberth, father of space travel, the teacher who inspired Wernher von Braun. They sought him out for conversation and discussion, and Erich welcomed them with joy, inviting them for an evening whisky or glass of red wine. But does a Graubünden hotel-keeper act this way? Certainly not, in the opinion of the Davos caucus. Guests are indeed welcome, but they must pay their own bills. 2. A hotelkeeper, as Davos defines him, says "Welcome" to his guests, caters to their physical needs, accepts payment and then says "Adieu"—but he writes no books, if you please. How dare he do such a thing!? 3. An hotelier goes a season or two, perhaps visiting relatives during his own vacations (because it's gratis), but does he undertake expensive trips around the world? Certainly not! 4. Finally, and this was by far

Erich's most critical deficiency, he was not a Graubündner, therefore obviously of an inferior race, to be tolerated but not accepted in Davos.

'And on top of all this that he could, so far removed from front desk, kitchen and bar, register a gigantic success with his books—that was simply unpardonable!'

Theo Bos, Däniken's shipmate when the latter was still short of the funds necessary to achieve his life's ambition, was thus in at the very beginning of EvD's efforts toward this goal.

'Two or three years before his first book appeared Erich was already convinced that only through facts, through authentic reports made right there in the respective localities, could he establish credibility among his future readers. He wanted to see for himself the puzzling and mysterious things about which he intended to write, and not rely on the reports of others. Only if one has been on the spot, and seen the pyramids for example, with his own eyes, or the ruins left by the Mayan culture—only then, Erich said to me, can he write about it and convincingly proclaim, "I was there, and I saw it!"

'But in order to bring all these plans to fruition, he needed money. And in order to realise money, he borrowed it. In no way did he ever intend that anyone who had lent him money should wind up short by a single penny. He once swore to me: "Theo, if the book is *not* a success and I have to work to repay all my debts, I'll work hard day and night. I'll go back to being a hotel waiter, because I can earn very well at that job. Then I'll pay back everyone to whom I owe money, even though at the moment I'm unable to."

'And in this sense Erich committed no criminal act, as far as I'm concerned!'

Otto von Däniken thinks similarly. Moroever, he is a businessman with both feet planted firmly on the ground.

'I don't believe that the amounts Erich borrowed at that time were excessive. As a hotelier with a ten-year lease whose house, as has been proved, was showing an increasing profit every year, credit was entirely within the framework of good business practice. The second question, whether he should have been extended credit on the basis of his future book, is a subjective one. Erich was absolutely convinced about his ideas and about the success of his book. But he also knew that in the unlikely event of failure, the hotel would become more successful in the next couple of years. So he had a second certainty to back up the first one. Under these circumstances it was thoroughly valid for him to incur further debts.

'Then there is the fact that when, in February 1968, Erich's first-born, *Erinnerungen an die Zunkuft* (*Chariots of the Gods*) appeared, and quickly advanced to Number One on best-seller lists, he signed over a blank power of attorney to his lawyer then, Dr Wasch, before taking off on his second major expedition. Wasch was to cover all obligations from the best-seller's proceeds. In this way all intention to defraud or damage anyone was excluded. The court, which later charged Erich with intention to defraud in spite of this plain fact, was a clique of stiff-necked ignoramuses. It whitewashed injustice in order to protect Kirchhofer and the District Attorney.'

In this latter-day Inquisition, this last 'witch-hunt', if I may call it that, Kirchhofer himself acted out the part of the 'Grey Eminence' in the background. Although it was repeatedly demanded of Prosecutor Padrutt that he be called as a witness, Kirchhofer was not summoned. Anyone present in the court would have known why. 'Had he been cross-examined by the accused, he would surely have given himself away,' surmised Rocholl/Roggersdorf in *Das seltsame Leben* . . . 'At the courtroom level Erich would have performed brilliantly—he knew the indictment almost word for word, and also the factual findings which had never been discussed.'

A few days after that 'black Friday' when sentence was pronounced on Däniken, the Zürich magazine *Blick* published the spontaneous protest of an indignant reader: 'They sentenced him as if he were a hardened criminal. At the same time in Glarus the murderer Heinrich Petermann also got three-and-a-half years, and after all, he had killed a man.'

They hastened to draw the convicted one out of circulation. Only five days after verbal announcement of the sentence (the written one followed almost two months later), and although the sentence was not yet legally in force, EvD was taken for 'execution of sentence' and transferred to Regensdorf penitentiary near Zürich. A petition for review bearing one thousand signatures of both prominent and ordinary people was rejected months later by the Federal Court in Bern. Not until August 18, 1971, after remission of two-thirds of the term of confinement, would the prison gates open again for Erich von Däniken.

Does a trauma remain after this bitter experience? Utz Utermann doubts it. 'He has a good set of nerves. I can only make assumptions here, for he scarcely speaks about it. But it would have been unnatural for the just person I came to know to completely forget the injury done him and the injustice he suffered. He was fairly well able to push it aside temporarily, and what helped him to do this was hard work—since he'd left the Regensdorf walls behind him, no day went by on which he didn't work like one possessed.'

This talent of EvD's that enabled him to bury in his subconscious things which burdened him physically and psychically also buoyed him up during his time in prison. Here is a typical illustration, reported by Walter Ernsting:

'While Erich was serving his term in Regensdorf I had an opportunity to visit him. Before this meeting we had been in constant touch with each other by post. Indeed, at Erich's suggestion, I had even written a novel based on his thesis (*The Day the Gods Died* has since appeared in English and French translations). He'd given me some good tips and helped me with editing and revision. Still, I was prepared to meet a pensive and dejected Däniken. So I stood there in the visiting-room with mixed feelings, partly happy to be seeing my friend again, partly filled with sympathy for his sad situation. How would this otherwise cheerful man appear today?

'I had braced myself against every eventuality except what actually occurred. Erich entered the room, saw me, hurried straight toward me. I extended a friendly hand which he took no notice of. He just ran up to me and shouted in his usual enthusiastic way, "Walter, I have some really wild ideas! When I get outside these walls, then I'll find the proof. I've been struck by several brain-waves, completely fantastic, and now I know where evidence might be found!" And that's how it went for the next few minutes. Wild ideas about this and that, some talk about my then-unfinished novel—then he belatedly discovered my still-extended hand and shook it heartily. I must say I was overjoyed to see Erich's energies undiminished in their intensity. Surely this spirit helped him to get through the difficult time in prison sound and well in mind and body.'

When the Federal Court in Bern rejected Erich von Däniken's clemency petition by a large majority, the one concerned didn't seem to be shaken. He only laughed over the short-sighted reason given by the appellate court—that Däniken had not only showed himself to be imprudent but had also exhibited no remorse for his 'deed'. In a letter to the St Gallen journalist Peter Schürmann EvD wrote, 'I'd rather drop dead than whine for clemency.'

Before rejection of the petition became known, a voice which can certainly not be dismissed, that of the Administrator of the Cantonal

Penitentiary at Regensdorf, Kurt Lendi, spoke up independently. Here are some excerpts from his letter:

... Although no conduct report has been officially requested, I feel impelled ... my personal experiences with von Däniken I make known on my own initiative. After he has worked in my office for more than eight months I believe I have come to know him sufficiently well to be able to describe him objectively.

In my thirty years of institutional experience I have hardly ever known a more work-enjoying, self-reliant and by nature agreeable co-worker. Although in the court verdict a 'deceitful and boastful type' is spoken of, whoever has known von Däniken over a long period can only testify to the contrary. Several months ago some of the staff of the Chur Penitentiary Sennhof were here for an inspection. We also discussed von Däniken, who spent a full year in Sennhof. Every official who had anything to do with von Däniken described him as correct, unassuming and basically decent.

I have arrived at the conviction that this man should not remain here any longer, and considering his severe sentence has atoned sufficiently. Carrying out the sentence in full seems to me senseless, and will only engender bitterness and hate in many hearts. Out of this conviction I would like to add my recommendation to the clemency petition.

'With these lines the Regensdorf Administrator unintentionally documented exactly what the High Court carefully passed over and took no notice of,' commented journalist Schürmann in the St Galler *Tagblatt*.

'Today perhaps it gives Erich a certain satisfaction to know that Examining Magistrate Kirchhofer, who presumably hoped to build his career on the "Däniken case", still sits in Davos on his little stool and, as I've heard from local people, still has made no connection and found few friends,' muses Utermann, and he may well be correct.

Erich von Däniken has indeed overcome the effects of the injustice done him, but in no way has he forgotten. His own story of the case, presented here for the first time, can be read in an Addendum to this book.

The sum total of the shameful legal campaign against one man whose fault was that he was above mediocrity, can be gleaned from the facts of a trial which would be unthinkable in Germany or Austria—or even elsewhere in Switzerland. Däniken's publisher Erwin Barth von

Wehrenalp was probably right when he stated at a coming-out party for the Press he gave upon Däniken's release, 'Such a trial is possible only in Graubünden—I believe even in Zürich it could never occur.'

As the *Spiegel* reporter defined the nature of the trial: '. . . nothing more . . . than a verbal execution . . .'

CHAPTER IX

Young Erich's 'Utopia'

With his mouth wide open, the boy stared at the apelike figure, naked but for a bearskin loincloth. It crouched in the cave entrance brandishing a giant club to frighten off intruders.

Before the boy was a tableau of the Life of Primitive Man; the Schaffhausen Museum had spared no pains to construct this realistic representation of a world long gone. The boy was Erich von Däniken, then twelve years old and unusually receptive to all that was mysterious and strange. He was completely fascinated, and even today remembers vividly the effect the 'weird illumination' lent to the scene. Probably during those years the seeds were sown which would later burgeon and grow and produce a record harvest of books.

Little Erich was certainly impressed, but his brain didn't accept what was offered unquestioningly. 'Was it really like that then?' he asked critically, his interest in mankind's past awakened. His imagination soared—and arrived at some extraordinary conclusions. Erich and his older brother Otto were avid readers of science-fiction novels; both of them felt as much at home in space as—well, as at home. The boys discussed the questions raised by these stories vehemently, conceived ideas about the future of the world—and returned with the speed of thought to prehistoric man.

'Of course Erich and I could never talk about these things with our father,' recalls Otto von Däniken. 'Papa was too conservative for such fantastic notions.' But their mother was not. The elderly widow still lives in Schaffhausen, the city where Otto Senior owned and managed a clothing business for many years.

In their mother Erich's older brother sees the source of that dream-world in which young Erich felt most secure. Lena von Däniken knew many fairy tales, and in the evenings would tell them to her children,

Leni, Trudi, Silvia, Otto and Erich. So as a small child, Erich's vivid imagination was already beginning to emerge.

'At first we read Utopian novels,' said brother Otto, talking about a taste they still share today. No wonder that both boys immersed themselves in the content of their mother's fairy stories. Otto von Däniken: 'I remember a youthful discussion where we asked ourselves whether Aladdin's Lamp couldn't have been some sort of television apparatus. And when we'd sometimes embark on adventurous "expeditions" into the woods, lurking in the background of our imaginings were the magic words "Open Sesame".'

In their early teens Otto and Erich collaborated in writing some adventure and science-fiction stories of their own, in which they both took roles. Today EvD dismisses them a little self-consciously as 'penny-dreadfuls'. His older brother: 'Our youthful adventure stories took place in Madagascar—which we knew only as a name on a map—on the Jungfrau-ridge in the Alps, and of course in the caves of Mars. Erich always wanted to be the hero, but I didn't mind that, because at the end of the story I always had to rescue him.' Grinning, Otto revealed that EvD had eventually ceased writing because his handwriting was so bad that no one could decipher it. But the lust for adventure and the taste for travel were already full-blown in young Erich. He read all the appropriate literature—Karl May, naturally, and the Swiss travel-writer Rene Gardi, whose works the fourteen-year-old devoured.

In Erich von Däniken the burning desire grew, to see and know the whole world. 'I want to travel and write, write and travel,' was fixed firmly in his mind. At first he limited this longing to minor attempts to run away from home. When he was only nine he departed into the wide world with his friend Lothar.

They tottered through the train corridor, leaped onto the open platform of one of the many cars heading for Singen, on the German border. The boys had a serious motive: Lothar's father, a German railwayman who lived with his family near the Schaffhausen station, hadn't returned home the evening before. This was in May 1945, during the last days of the war. Erich was ready and willing to help Lothar search for his father. In order not to excite suspicion, they sang loudly 'Nun ade, du mein lieb Heimatland,' which made them feel very important. Neither Erich nor Lothar had the slightest twinge of conscience. Well-provided with food, they rode the train to within 500 metres of the customs barrier and jumped off, intending to sneak across the border. With clever foresight, the adventurers had supplied themselves with a small basket; should a customs officer approach them, they would say they were gathering mushrooms. Like stalking Indians, the two boys slunk through the brush. After dark they would surely be able to smuggle themselves unseen across the border into Germany.

At home things were in an uproar. Both boys' mothers were worried almost out of their minds, and Papa Däniken growled thunderously, 'When Erich gets back I'll beat him half to death!' But the days went by with no trace of the runaways.

They had meanwhile succeeded in reaching Singen, and were caught up helplessly in the turmoil of the end of the war. Valiantly they stuck with their mission, inquiring after Lothar's father. They found and followed a clue leading north to Bad Triberg. But they didn't get that far—French occupation troops became suspicious, picked up the boys and turned them over to Swiss border officials, who without more ado, threw them in jail—in separate cells for a whole long night. EvD remembers with a shudder: 'The next morning we heard footsteps, and I was horrified to recognise my father's voice. I was dreadfully afraid—I can still picture the scene vividly. My father simply walked into the cell and stood there not saying a word, not a single word. I also remained silent, except for the chattering of my teeth.'

Both boys got off easily—their parents' joy (Lothar's father had meanwhile returned) over their safe return overcame all their anger. The adventure had lasted ten days.

EvD's fear of his father was not unfounded; master tailor Otto von Däniken was a strict and pious man. If Erich was disobedient the authoritarian parent banished him to the coal-cellar. EvD has also kept that memory fresh all these years. As good as his relationship with his mother was and is—he visits her regularly—so was it a strained one with his father. Däniken has never forgiven him for his excessive discipline. 'I never looked upon my father as a friend,' he says today.

The Frankfurt psychologist Knut Hebert ('All psychologists have the same dirty minds,' says Erich, staving off undesired analyses) believes he has discovered in this paternal severity the clue to Däniken's later hypotheses about astronaut-gods. 'The object of his first book *Chariots of the Gods?*, was no more than patricide. Our Father who art in Heaven is dead. Our Gods are astronauts from unknown stars,' he theorised. How lucky we are to have psychologists; they know the solution to every mystery.

Anyway, it's certain that relations between the religious father and his inquisitive son continued to disintegrate. Especially after the clothier placed both Erich and Otto in the Catholic College of Saint-Michel, where EvD soon began to clash with his teachers of religion.

Erich von Däniken was not a heretic. He wanted to believe—but theological dogma had to be explained to him logically. He asked the Abbot, 'Why is this translated so differently? When Jesus was interrogated by the high priest, He was asked, "Are you the Son of God?" In the Latin version he's supposed to have answered, "I am." But the Greek translation has him replying, "You say it." Now which is right?'

Däniken couldn't accept the ambiguity of such translations. In the Latin version the Son of God persisted in His position. But in the Greek tradition His answer simply returned the high priest's question to Him. There were two entirely different interpretations of what He said. The Abbot refused to answer. But in Däniken's school report under 'Diligence' is found: 'Good, but talkative.'

Doubts grew in young Erich's heart; he missed the *logic* of it. 'For the first year and a half everything went along fairly well,' says brother Otto. But then the situation began to change. The main trouble was that the relationship between the doubter Erich and his strict believer father became more tense. If the master tailor had known what 'heretical' reading material his younger son was secretly consuming, a family thunderstorm would have been inevitable.

From the nearby university library EvD borrowed Nietzsche's *Antichrist*, as well as works by Kant and Schopenhauer. They belonged on his obligatory book-list, as did Haeckel's *Abstammungslehre*, which was in absolute disharmony with the childish legend of paradise taught in his religion class.

Erich avoided any discussion with his father, knowing that nothing could be gained by it. The situation continued thus for some time until one day it all burst out of him. He overcame his fear of his stern father, provoked beyond endurance by the latter's narrow-minded views. After completing three years at college, by now a seventeen-year-old, he posed some disagreeable questions for the first time.

Otto von Däniken: 'There were some bitter quarrels, which often ended angrily, for naturally father had the last word. Not that he would ever have succeeded in convincing Erich, but his method of argument, using a raised voice and paternal pressure was overpowering.'

Däniken Senior religiously observed his religious duties. Each evening the rosary was told, and Sundays the whole family marched to church. The father knew a proven method to get his children to concentrate on services; at the midday meal they had to tell him exactly what the priest's sermon had dealt with. EvD's elder brother: 'Erich and I of course had other things in mind. When the service reached a certain point we stole back—often too late—behind the droning mass of worshippers in order to hear the sermon. But if something went wrong there was a terrible scene, and the threat of Holy Retribution was suspended over our heads.'

Knut Hebert, the psychologist quoted earlier, again has something to add. In the strict, religious boarding school EvD had come to know 'Maria, the chaste maiden', and his childhood had been completely dominated by his beloved mother, whom he trusted implicitly. As a result—maintains the Frankfurt psychologist—Däniken's attitude toward sex was influenced. 'He has none. He is a narcissist—a man who loves only himself. Therefore his relationship to women is "rather complicated".'

Certainly the stay in Saint-Michel didn't entirely agree with the inquiring student. Knut Hebert finds: 'Repressive education opened a new dimension for Erich. Uncertainty about the nature of the sexes slipped in, and his own impulses shook him in the dimness of the confessional. The college world was masculine. The abbots lived in celibacy, the pupils in their heart's confusion. Fifteen-year-old Erich was kissed by a comrade behind the abbey wall . . .'

Erich von Däniken in reluctant remembrance: 'I felt nothing—the other one got red! Anyway, I wasn't mature then, not in any respect, and I believe that—especially where sex is concerned—I got my hang-ups through such squalid education and upbringing.'

In *Das seltsame Leben* . . . Rocholl and Roggersdorf quote extracts from Swiss 'Student Regulations' issued by the National Council. They delineate the narrow limits within which EvD could move when he entered Saint-Michel in the spring of 1949.

1. Religion is the foundation of education and of the College curriculum. . . . Instruction begins and closes with prayer.

2. Study is a moral obligation for students, their duty and responsibility.

8. Idleness, carelessness and unsatisfactory grades could entail expulsion. A student who . . . does not achieve an average mark of 4 [6 was highest, 1 lowest] may be requested to leave the College.

15. The reading or possession of books, newspapers and other

publications which oppose Religion, good morals and the social order is strictly prohibited.

These dogmatic directives received no respectful response from an inquiring spirit like the youthful Erich von Däniken.

On the last day of school in 1952, the Prefect admonished his pupils to live each day so that at any hour they could stand before God pure in heart because they had never doubted His word and had always believed in Him—'Then you will be among those who on Judgment Day will stand at God's right hand. . . .'

Erich knew then that the *left* side would be reserved for him, for he was filled with doubt. Otto von Däniken: 'On the way home Erich spoke not a word to me, contrary to his usual habit. He just stared through the compartment window, his mind and spirit far away.'

EvD couldn't believe that the Prefect's wise, almighty God wanted him to accept such childlike and illogical doctrines. Hadn't he given his most intelligent creations their intellect and understanding so that they could use it? Was it forbidden for them to question, to doubt? On that day Erich decided: 'His' God, whom he accepted, in whom he truly believed, did not advocate blind faith.

Twenty-two years later Erich von Däniken, who meanwhile had become a best-selling author, wrote his reflections about the true nature of the essence locked up in the soul. The book *Erscheinungen* (*Miracles of the Gods*) was not a typical 'Däniken', for it dealt with his conception of faith and religious dogma; his interpretation of apparently-unexplainable 'miracles'. Earlier, in his third best seller, *Aussaat und Kosmos* (*The Gold of the Gods*), EvD had asked provocatively:

Should we blow up temples, demolish churches?
No, never.
Wherever men gather to glorify the Creator, they feel a comforting and strengthening sense of community. As if stirred by the piercing note of a tuning fork, a collective sensation of something sublime vibrates throughout the room. Temples and churches are places for contemplation, houses for the communal praise of that indefinable IT which for lack of a better term we have learned to call God. These places of congregation are necessary, but all else is superfluous.

That EvD propagates atheistic notions, as some sources insinuate, is simply untrue. He believes in a Supreme Being today just as he always has. That this incomprehensible Something proceeds logically in every phase of his actions, Däniken is absolutely certain. But religions deal with matters of Faith—another subject entirely. This is how his thoughts on religion have developed from that childhood period to the present day.

'The IT of Erich von Däniken is the spirit of all the worlds, something like the key to a greater truth,' recognises psychologist Knut Hebert, and the god-seeker is searching for this truth. Hebert appears to be fascinated by the doggedness with which Däniken searches for conclusive proof of his assertions: the *spaceship* which the astronauts in whom he believes brought to the earth from somewhere in the Universe. 'So in his own fashion he is happy, and no case for a psychiatrist.'

The idea that extra-terrestrial visitors could once have set foot on this planet first came to EvD when he was nine years old. In February 1944, he saw an American bomber make an emergency landing in Schaffhausen. Eight men climbed out of the huge, sinister machine and walked silently past him 'like beings from another world'—from another star.

That event, it seems, is typical of EvD's experiences and perceptions. He is susceptible to the threatening, the massive, the uncanny, the archaic, and impressions gained at such moments solidify, so that they reinforce a system of convictions already in existence.

When he was twenty, the Utopian novels of a certain Clark Darlton first came into his hands, in which the author identified mysterious occurrences in mankind's prehistory with the visits of extra-terrestrial intelligent beings whom the ignorant earthlings regarded as gods. This Clark Darlton was no other than Walter Ernsting, who was to become EvD's friend twelve years later, and who was indirectly a forerunner of the Swiss researcher.

In a casual three-way conversation we discovered that I too had been a Darlton-fan in the middle fifties, and had read his science-fiction hypotheses of visits by strange astronaut-gods with increasing enthusiasm. Ernsting's writings had sowed seeds which had sprouted years later in Erich and me, wholly unbeknownst to one another, as Däniken and I were not acquainted at the time. We were three friends who had been linked by an intellectual bridge at a time when none knew the others. That war experience, the emergency landing of an American plane in Schaffhausen, had stimulated small Däniken to later achievements. Although through some mix-up this very same Swiss town of Schaffhausen suffered a terrible blow on April 1, 1944—when American bombs fell on it, killing forty-two people—that did not deter Däniken and his comrades from making voyages of discovery.

'Erich was once again the boss,' related his brother Otto, who went along as the gang eagerly collected bomb-splinters or clambered among the ruins of buildings. 'Erich and I felt reasonably safe, even as we climbed stairs to the third floor of a bomb-demolished restaurant. Suddenly there was an ear-splitting crash—the steps we'd just climbed had fallen into rubble. We were marooned on the third floor; climbing down was out of the question. Luckily our cries for help were heard, and a fire-engine with a long ladder arrived shortly after. We were dropped off at our house and the firemen reminded Papa of his parental responsibilities.

'Naturally there was hell to pay, and we were both required to promise never to undertake such climbing expeditions again. Erich promised his father solemnly that he'd avoid *this* ruined place, the sly lad knowing full well that there were other bombed houses in Schaffhausen. So he had a clear conscience about keeping his promise.'

Otto von Däniken still recalls with pleasure the uncountable pranks he and his brother devised during their childhood years, and that understandably it was mostly little Erich who set the pace.

'As boys we often had house- and street-battles, but they were waged with no violence and much laughter. Boys and girls on one side engaged in friendly rivalry with girls and boys on the other side. I don't mean ball-games—it was more like capturing your opponents and making them pay a forfeit.

'Erich took these "battles" a little too seriously. Sometimes he'd cut school classes for several afternoons so that he could make preparations for the next battle undisturbed. For instance, once he built a cannon from a cardboard tube and loaded it with fireworks. He then mounted a gun-carriage on a cart and rushed it through "enemy" territory. What happened next happened very quickly. A projectile trailing brightly-coloured stars unexpectedly went through old Mrs Hausamann's ground-floor window. Her curtains caught fire.'

While his friends took to their heels, little Däniken showed calm control and presence of mind. He raced to the window, jumped up on the sill and tore down the burning curtains. They were completely ruined, but a real conflagration had been prevented. However, the evil-doer couldn't prevent a sound thrashing from being administered by his furious father, who had to pay for replacing Mrs Hausamann's carbonised curtains.

'From then on my brother changed his battle tactics,' laughs Otto von Däniken, and remembered as well a thrilling experience which scared both of them out of their skins.

'One afternoon Erich and I had played truant again, and he talked me into going with him to the nearby wood to cut arrows for our archery sets. We were in the so-called "Enge-Wald" when we suddenly saw behind a tree not ten metres away a strange man holding a pistol. We noted neither his height nor clothing, let alone his complexion or the colour of his eyes. We had only one thought—flight. But where? In fear and panic we ducked behind "our" tree. The strange hand holding the pistol seemed to be pointing threateningly at us. Only Heaven could save us. Not yet thirteen years old, I cried out desperately:

"Help us, Mary, Mother of God!"

And next to me Erich added, loud and clear:

"We're here in the wood!"

He was apparently in doubt as to whether the Mother of God knew our location.'

CHAPTER X

Sowing for the Future

He likes to surround himself with something of an aura of mystery; Erich von Däniken knows what is expected of someone in his position. And when he does let the suspicion creep in, that he is really 'the most important and most brilliant satirist in German literature for at least a century' (Wunderlich), he comments ambiguously, leaving all possible interpretations open ('The answer is yes and no'). EvD also attempts to give the content and the ideas in his books an air of ambiguity.

A favourite topic of conversation is the book titles he has chosen. Däniken says they are the external representation of a series, arranged in the form of an inverted pyramid. Actually, only his first three books belong to this cycle so far. The fourth book, *Meine Welt in Bildern* (*My World in Pictures*), although enriched with some new flashes of inspiration from the god-seeker, was essentially a photographic supplement to the global mysteries presented in his earlier books. The fifth, *Erscheinungen* (*Miracles of the Gods*), was entirely out of the frame, consisting principally of mysticism and miracles. And the next, *Besucher aus dem Kosmos* (*Visitors from the Cosmos*), was a collection of the most interesting portions of EvD's first three books, compiled by his editor Wilhelm Roggersdorf (Utz Utermann).

So his three earlier published works, plus the one just released

Erinnerungen an die Zukunft
Zurück zu den Sternen
Aussaat und Kosmos
Beweise

—form the pyramid.

The last, *Beweise* (*Proofs*), says Däniken, is the culmination of his endeavours as investigator and author—the reward for his exertions.

For his process to 'proofs', EvD is indebted to his readers above all, but also to a sceptical and often hostile Science. It has truly been a major undertaking for the best-selling author—a voyage toward a daring objective; but one which Däniken could really no longer evade, even had he wished to. The public (both experts and laymen) finally demanded something concrete from him, no more theories and hypotheses—they had gradually lost their persuasive power.

Among the group of authors who write on similar themes—and they are legion—EvD is the 'tip of the iceberg'. The others bloom and thrive (or starve) at a level of popularity far below Däniken's. So upon him fall the scurrilous and abusive attacks of the 'non-believers'. He must show his colours and take up the role of champion for his writing colleagues. But *woe*!—if his *Beweise* is nonsense, then woe to all the others; they must all sink together. So strange as it may sound, von Däniken carries on his investigative labours not for himself alone. In spirit they are all, the many 'god-researchers' in America, England, Europe and elsewhere, in the same boat. Will EvD triumph?

I know that those who have travelled with him along a common way believe that he will. They know his obstinate determination to reach that aimed-for goal.

'He's a typical Aries,' says brother Otto. 'If he realises that something can be achieved and he wants to achieve that something, he does so. And he does so with a sort of missionary zeal—he has a way of winning through without giving offence to anyone.'

But will he find *his* proof, *his* evidence? Otto von Däniken is convinced of it. 'If Erich lives another twenty years, then certainly the answer is "yes". Simply because he doesn't give up; it would run counter to his character. His style is to set himself a goal and then strive toward it. Of course the necessary financial means must be available—and health. As long as he has both, his goal will be reached. That is his strength of character. And when one day one or both of those factors drop out, Erich will probably try to enlist younger men in the battle. But give up—not until his last breath, I'm sure of that.'

One who probably knows more about all this than any other, but who in his employer's interest is keeping silent for the present, is his secretary Willi Dünnenberger. For two months in 1975 he travelled with EvD through India, Pakistan, and Turkey, and—as he mysteriously intimates —Däniken tracked down visible *proofs* which are reported on in his new book *Beweise*. Something new must be expected to emerge from an 18,000-kilometre Range Rover expedition, Dünnenberger's judgment is not entirely uncritical; in a discussion I had with him before he set out on that long journey, he said, 'Personally, I believe that Erich will find proofs. It's surely clear that in future he must offer more than books containing only circumstantial evidence—people will stop buying them. More is expected of him. For that reason I believe that in the next three years Erich will be compelled to find the damned proof.'

'I think the fact that space travel exists at all, that it's now an established actuality, favours Erich finding his proof some day,' says Theo Bos of his old companion. 'Much can be said to support this assumption —that there were ancient astronauts is a logical solution to the riddles Erich poses. Consider the ruins of the Mayan culture; aren't they an obvious example? Why were whole cliffs hacked out and steps cut into them—steps that are upside-down? Logical answer: At some time or other, perhaps through a natural cataclysm, the cliffs were turned upside-down. Or will someone try to tell me that the steps were cut out of the cliff inverted like that? But position aside, what's even more provocative about these steps is their gigantic size. They don't seem to have been fabricated by the hand of man.

'Therefore I believe: either Mankind had a highly-developed culture in the distant past, or earth really received visits from space. Now if the people here on earth uncountable years ago were intelligent enough to construct such things—the remains of which we find today—why and how were all these things wiped out? Was their intelligence so great that they were destroyed by their own achievements? Worldwide suicide, as it were? I don't believe it. Had these early intelligences really been in a position to depopulate an entire planet, they would have carried out their work of destruction more thoroughly. Then there wouldn't have been any so-called "souvenirs" remaining. Traces of earlier civilisations wouldn't exist. So I believe, because such remains *do* exist, that once, long ago, intelligent beings from *outside* visted our earth, and that these strangers deliberately left such "souvenirs" behind, as visible evidence of their having been here. Erich von Däniken has found these indications in great number, and that's why I'm convinced that he'll discover his irrefutable proof.'

Among the heterogeneous multitude of the 'convinced' we find the former sceptic, NASA engineer Josef Blumrich. He belongs to that uncommon kind of scientist who conducts himself according to Francis Bacon's sentiment that everything is not permissible, but anything is possible. Blumrich hopes that Däniken's project succeeds. 'If any of us has the chance, he is the one, Erich has not only the enthusiasm but also the funds to transform his plans into deeds. On top of that he has the will-power and the physical endurance—and all these things consolidate his chances for success.

'The criteria as to whether what he finds is really traceable to an extra-terrestrial culture, or what is just as possible, to an early highly-developed earth culture—these criteria must be examined on a purely scientific basis. They would be matters for physicists and engineers, to be analysed dispassionately and with no public sensationalism. Those people who then devote themselves to examining Däniken's evidence scientifically need three things in order to be able to work undisturbed —time, money and tranquillity.'

On the other hand, Hans Neuner hopes that EvD is allowed to track down the indications of space visitors which he claims to have found— 'They're there indeed!'—in peace, and without putting himself in danger. 'That would be ideal for him. That there seems to be something to this whole set of concepts is shown by the attempts of influential institutions to "cover up" various puzzling things, mystifying occurrences they don't allow to be publicised. There are the UFO-phenomena and certain strange archaeological finds, to cite two examples. Then think about the mysterious disappearances of aircraft and ships in the "Bermuda Triangle". From either silence or denial one learns nothing. And what about the various libraries where no one may enter, for instance the Vatican Library? What treasures slumber there, and what revolutionary changes could result if they were publicised? I'll bet really wild things would happen on that day!'

Perry Rhodan, the alias of author Walter Ernsting, has the same opinion. He remembers how back in 1934 he read and was impressed by the Utopian adventure series 'Sun Koh' from the pen of Freder von Holk. These tales dealt with Atlantis, extra-terrestrial spaceships 10,000 years ago, and the attempt of strange 'Gods' to shape the cultural development of this planet to their own pattern. Ernsting sees therein an anticipation of *Chariots of the Gods?*, but suggests some things which might limit Däniken's investigative zeal. Of course Ernsting has no doubt that EvD will continue to search for the final proof in future, 'Only I'm not always sure that Erich is searching for it in the right place. This is grounded in the possibility that such proofs (for I believe that there are several to be discovered) may lie, or perhaps hover, in locations not easily reached. At least not with the technical means available to us at present. Such proofs could be on the ocean floor, or just as likely, in nearby space. Here I go along with Däniken's reflections, that perhaps the reason we haven't yet found anything tangible is because we're simply not mature enough to be *allowed* to find it.'

Here Ernsting sees the essential question about Däniken's future endeavours. Should EvD not find these proofs, this evidence, during his lifetime, then he may have already reached the peak of his writing career, if indeed there is nothing else explosively new to discover. But if proofs should be found, says Ernsting, the situation would be entirely different. 'Then the real high-point of his career is still before him.'

I thought it would be interesting to pose this question of EvD's writing future to 'Anti-Däniken' Gerhard Gadow. As expected, the Berliner gave his answer with typical caution. He couldn't reply decisively to my question, whether Däniken had already, or not yet, reached the zenith of success 'because that depends essentially on whether he's successful in the near future in inflicting the final, or a convincing proof on his followers and opponents'.

No, perhaps diplomacy is not Gadow's weakness.

Utz Utermann sees the Däniken-situation entirely differently. His feeling is that the burden of proof has been misplaced. His plea is to look at the affair from a new aspect: 'They say, "Däniken should prove that other-worldly cosmonauts have visited the earth." But why isn't it admissible to turn the tables—let them show us some evidence that they were *not* here!'

Däniken has provided numerous clues, but the so-called counterevidence is little more than a blanket rejection, in line with the principle 'Because it can not be, it may not be'.

EvD has long been an inquisitive and studious novice in every possible branch of the various sciences. But it seems unfair to me when a specialist in some scientific field takes a portion of Däniken's theory which happens to fall in his sphere and tears it to shreds. Naturally these experts have a thorough and detailed knowledge, and can easily stamp Däniken as a blunderer or convict him of an erroneous interpretation— but Erich has never maintained nor written that he's at home in every branch of knowledge.

More weight should be given to the phenomenon of a self-educated man who has started a wave of second-thoughts—who has awakened scepticism about an array of tacitly-accepted dogmas dating back to the eighteenth century and beyond. And that in an era which knows only personal and political confrontation he brings forward topics that stir men deeply. Discussion is a unifying influence, and Däniken has contributed his bit to that unification. Isn't that an enormous plus for him?

Utermann believes and trusts that in the long run Däniken's positive effect will be assessed at its true value. EvD's wife Elisabeth also expresses trust in her husband. Although she openly confesses to not having read all of Erich's books, she naturally hopes he is successful in his pursuit of the final proof. But with the caution of a realist whose feet rest solidly on Mother Earth, she limits her enthusiasm :'But that of course can't be predicted. Does anyone know for sure how the world will develop in the future? Isn't it conceivable that one day God will know what's going on?'

But the world situation disturbs Däniken's publisher von Wehrenalp not at all. He continues to sail before the wind of controversy raised by his most successful author. He anticipates that Däniken's latest and current book *Beweise*, one especially significant in content, will also prove to be most profitable in sales.

Is a new Däniken-boom in the offing? Will there be further expeditions, exhausting lecture-tours in Europe and abroad, television and radio, taped interviews? Proofs aside, for how long can this short, husky man withstand the enormous burden? Doesn't all this imperil his health?

To his family this is an ever-present worry. Mrs von Däniken knows well that her husband doesn't take enough exercise. 'When he's at home, I at least try to take him along for a short run daily. Probably the only light athletic exercise Erich gets. He knows the danger in overloading his body, and has a physical examination more or less regularly. If I express myself strongly regarding health matters he usually accepts it. That is, if it doesn't have to do with the dentist.'

Brother Otto also knows what's what. 'The stress is there, without a doubt, and I often fear that Erich overestimates himself. Indeed stress isn't just "work", it's both a mental and physical burden.

'Here's the way it is with me. I can sit in an armchair and puff on my pipe—outwardly calm. But I'm still under stress; my brain tries somehow to channel and digest all the exciting happenings of the bygone hours. In this sense Erich is under continuous stress. And he doesn't give his body nearly enough physical exertion. His outward appearance doesn't concern him one way or the other. He pays little heed to admonitions to keep himself in shape, and when he does, it's with a tolerant smile. As if he was saying, "Just leave me in peace and take care of your own physique."

'We have several doctors in the family who one and all urge Erich to lose some weight. His reply is always the same: "A hungry stomach produces nervous mental activity. Instead of sermonising, invent some low-calorie foods that are also delicious." '

Däniken admits that journeys like the one to India, Pakistan and Turkey, often demand the last reserves of his strength; but he risks them because 'they fulfil my youthful dreams about adventures in strange lands'. In the *Hör Zu* series 'Auf neuen rätselhaften Spüren' (On the Track of New Mysteries) he confessed to tempting fate:

'I like to be challenged by unforeseen, inextricable situations. I want to win through, and I *do* win through. . . .'

Whatever happens to him, Däniken has taken care of the future. Some years ago he deposited a batch of his semen in an American seminal bank, to be stored deep-frozen. He told psychologist Knut Hebert about it: 'They talked until my head spun, saying they already had semen from various scientists and eminent persons, and how important it was to preserve these specimens for future genetic crossings. They kept talking and urging for so long that I finally said okay. I received seven hundred dollars for it.'

Disregarding the fact that he has been interested in the gene-mutation field for a long time, and has reported on 'retort-babies'—'Three are scientifically recognised, but there are probably two hundred'—he is seldom able to say 'no' when it's pointed out to him what distinguished company he's in.

To give another instance of this: on February 12, 1975, the University of Bolivia conferred upon the Swiss god-seeker the title 'Doctor honoris causa'. The corresponding degree, a document confirming this distinction, was ceremoniously presented to the newly-ordained *Doctor* Erich von Däniken at his home in Bonstetten by a delegation from the Bolivian university.

This isn't the only honour he has received; at the Second World Conference of the Ancient Astronaut Society held in Zürich in late May of 1975, EvD received from the hand of the Society's chairman, Gene Phillips, a 'Decoration of Merit in the Field of Astro-Archaeology.' This was the first such award presented by the worldwide organisation; it was well-deserved and honestly earned by Däniken. The Society have since held their third Conference in Crikvenica, Jugoslavia, and their fourth, in 1977, in Rio de Janeiro.

Although not the first author in the area of astronaut-gods, but certainly a pioneer in this new and controversial para-scientific field, Däniken battles on imperturbably through the thickets of narrow-minded arrogance with which many of his contemporaries surround themselves. The filming of two of his books has helped to sustain his popular appeal. In 1970 'Chariots of the Gods' was shown all over the world, dubbed in many languages; and since Spring of 1976 'Mysteries of the Gods' has been playing in theatres everywhere.

So Däniken's name is still on everyone's lips. As a result, hopes are high that his activities, his search for evidence, will end successfully. Will he satisfy those expectations? EvD is sure of it, and bases his conviction on a guardedly-intimated, extra-sensory talent of his which he calls 'espern' (from ESP, extra-sensory perception).

This is an extract from a magazine interview with Erich von Däniken (*Der Spiegel*, No. 12, March 19, 1973):

Spiegel: Can you place your first ESP-experience?
Däniken: That was almost 18 years ago.
Spiegel: You were in boarding school?
Däniken: Right.
Spiegel: And this unique experience convinced you that astronauts from other stars . . .
Däniken: To my mind, from solar systems in other galaxies . . .
Spiegel: . . . so this youthful experience in Fribourg was decisive to these perceptions?
Däniken: Correct.
Spiegel: Did this ESP-experience implant in you the solid certainty of a landing of strange astronauts on earth?
Däniken: At first I wasn't sure. What I experienced then was so unusual that—but please, I'd rather not talk any more about it . . .
Spiegel: Then ESP is an essential source of your cognition?
Däniken: A source which has brought me to the definite conviction that the earth was visited by extra-terrestrial astronauts. I know it. And I know that in the near future an event will take place which will prove that I'm right . . .

Whatever you think of this, it is possible that EvD's announced 'event' may have already occurred. I refer to a book written by a German television correspondent in Rio de Janeiro, Karl Brugger, which was published in Spring of 1976. This strange volume, *Die Chronik von Akakor* (*Chronicles of Akakor*), is based mainly on tales of the young Indian chieftain Tatunca Nara of the isolated Amazonian forest tribe Ugha Mongulala.

Brugger, who holds degrees in Sociology and Modern History, has become an authority on South American Indian cultures. He won the confidence of Tatunca Nara, a son of the Indian high chief Sinkaia, whose Ugha Mongulala lineage is also linked to the Dacca and Haisha tribes. The young warrior, whose trust in the civilisation of the 'white barbarians' was rather limited, told Brugger about a secret book of his people, those very *Chronicles of Akakor*, Akakor being the former capital city of the Ugha Mongulala. Described in the *Chronicles* as the history of this Indian tribe from the year one to the present, a period encompassing more than 10,000 (!) years. Tatunca Nara vouches for the authenticity of the data, and if he's not serving up an imaginative invention—very unlikely, for he'd have nothing on which to base it— then handed down in the *Chronicles* are stories that verify the long-ago visit of strange astronauts to this earth.

Here is short extract from this extraordinary world:

These are the tidings. This is the history of the chosen servants. In the beginning all was chaos. Men lived like animals, without reason and without knowledge, without laws and without tilling the soil. They went naked on all fours until the Gods came—they brought men the light.

We do not know the place from where the strange Gods came, only the name they gave it. From the generation-telling of our forefathers we know it as 3000 years before Year Zero. Then suddenly gold-bright ships appeared in the sky. Powerful signal lights illumined the ground. The earth shook, and thunder sounded across the hills. Men bowed their heads in awe before the mighty strangers who had come to take possession of the earth.

The strangers called their home *Shverta*, a far-distant world in the deeps of space. Their ancestors lived there. They came away in order to bring their knowledge to other worlds. Our priests say it was a powerful empire, existing on many planets, as numberless as grains of sand. They say that the two worlds, Earth and this world of our early ancestors, meet every six thousand years. Then the Gods will return.

Now let us make a big leap back to that part of the first chapter where we dealt with the mysterious Ecuadorean caves described by Däniken in his book *The Gold of the Gods*, upon which orthodox scientists heaped ridicule and scorn. These caves and tunnels exist, and there are similar systems elsewhere than in South America. Now according to the *Chron-*

icles there are 13 (!) subterranean cities 'buried deep in the mountains called the Andes', and their ground-plan duplicates the constellation of Shverta, the home of the Gods. High-chief's son Tatunca Nara asserts that four of the cities are occupied by his people, the others having been deserted long ago.

If what Karl Brugger presents in his extraordinary book can be substantiated, it's clearly sensational. Then it would be more than a hypothesis, it would be *The Proof*.

For in addition, the author's Indian informant reports that in the underground temple vaults of Akakor there is *technical equipment*, such as a flying disk, and another unusual vehicle that can 'move over water and mountains'. These things are kept by the Ugha Mongulala priests, who describe them as 'heirlooms from the Gods'.

Here is another excerpt from Brugger's book:

> The flying disk is shining gold in colour, but made of some other unknown metal. There is room inside for two passengers. It has neither sail nor rudder. But our priests say that Lhasa (one of the Gods) can fly in it faster than the fastest eagle, and that it moves as light among the clouds as a leaf in the wind.
>
> The strange vehicle is likewise puzzling. It is a large silvery pod with seven long legs, three in front and four at the rear. They are movable, and look like bent bamboo stalks. At their ends are rollers the size of a water-lily. . . .

This is from a letter of Erich von Däniken's to Walter Ernsting, about EvD's ESP-ability and his search for proof:

> I'm looking on this globe for a sign, a symbol, perhaps written characters of some kind. I'll find this sign, first on a spherical object, then again and again everywhere, after I've recognised it the first time.
>
> When I'm standing before the sign or in its vicinity, I'll know that this is what I'm looking for, this is the key. But right now as I type these lines I don't know what it looks like, although I've 'seen' it uncountable times. . . .

According to the statements of Tatunca Nara, priests in the underground temples guard relics bearing mysterious written characters from the era of the Gods, indecipherable to them.

> There are 1400 symbols, which from their arrangement in rows and columns must hold several discrete items of information. . . .

Is Däniken on the threshold of the most productive period of his investigative career? Will he perhaps be allowed access to the subterranean cities of the Ugha Mongulala? Will his alleged extra-sensory ability be of use to him there? In a conversation with psychologist Knut Hebert, EvD described openly the means he takes to 'espern'; 'I look upward and inward and try to see a black patch. On this black screen, the pictures emerge.'

Now whether EvD's Psi-effect is genuine or imaginary, it certainly is useful in finding authentic evidence of the once-upon-a-time visit of intelligent beings from another world. The *Chronicles of Akakor* seems to offer worthwhile clues. Will the god-seeker follow them?

If the answer is *yes*, his family will see him even less than they do now. From conversations with his wife and with his brother, two very clear but completely different views emerge. They contradict one another— or do they?

Elisabeth von Däniken is in accord with her Erich's choice of calling, 'because every day that he's home I see how happy and fulfilled he is. And that's the most essential thing.'

'Ebet' immediately answered 'Yes!' when I asked her whether she'd still have married Erich, if she'd known what the present situation would be.

'This is how it is,' said she, 'in every marriage there has to be a certain amount of adaptation. And there are drawbacks to everything. Keeping that in mind, our marriage is no better nor worse than any other.'

Even less emotional and more matter-of-fact was Otto von Däniken's assessment of his brother's personal future, with reference to his more intensive search for evidence.

'With regard to Elisabeth and Erich I see no problem. In other marriages this would be an impossible situation, but not for people with their characteristics. This union has survived the lower depths of the arrest, accusation and imprisonment. And it continues to stand the test now that things go well financially, and both of them can afford whatever they desire. Erich's wife is often at home alone, without feeling too much pain over her husband's absence. As she's told me herself, she compensates for it by her pleasure in her two dogs, with colleagues in the Kennel and the Pistol Club, and finally in her home, where she has to look after her fourteen-year-old daughter. I know from my brother that he's repeatedly asked her and even pressured her to come along on trips. She doesn't want to—she likes it better at home.'

Theoretically this situation could change in future, for Däniken's daughter Cornelia is now attending a boarding school, and there's more freedom, if no more desire, for Ebet to travel.

Otto again: 'Erich is really a "family- and home-loving man", but to a very limited extent. When he's been away for a time, he starts to yearn for domestic life and home cooking. And don't forget the wine cellar. But after two weeks at home, he starts to feel the pull of the world outside, a sort of reverse nostalgia. You could liken him to a professional seaman in this respect.'

Regarding the stability of Däniken's marriage, Otto says: 'In my view it's solider than many others, and will remain so at least until Cornelia is grown. Then I could quite imagine them—knowing the generosity and tolerance of both Elisabeth and Erich—separating for awhile with complete affection, each going their own way. To experience the so-called "second springtime". This would be in no way a divorce—more of a festivity.'

One is inclined to believe these words. Uncommon people are predestined to do uncommon things. This match should be measured by other standards—it isn't comparable with run-of-the-mill matrimony; it's also a sentimental partnership. What Erich and Ebet have welded together is often only recognisable by tiny, apparently inconsequential signs. Like the fact that earlier Erich rechristened all his travelling companions in Europe and abroad 'Peter'. Why? Perhaps because the god-seeker perceived in each of his young companions an image of his son. That son, Peterli, who would now be sixteen, suffocated in his crib when scarcely two months old. Isn't such a reminiscence more enlightening than the malicious, unfounded, insinuations made by some of his enemies?

It is possible Erich von Däniken stands on the brink of a new discovery which could overturn the scientific conception of the world, or at least change it. Meanwhile he must resign himself to having his convictions opposed and ridiculed; but I can't help suspecting that he still holds something in reserve, something with the power of vindicating himself—as in the case of Heinrich Schliemann and the discovery of Troy.

A new scientific truth never makes its way in such fashion that its opponents are convinced and declare it to be correct, but rather by the dying-out of its opponents, and by making the upcoming generation conversant with that truth from the start.

This was said by none other than Max Planck, Nobel Prizewinner in Physics, and he said it with reference to a few bad experiences of his own with narrow-minded, egotistical 'colleagues'.

In his time even the great Johann Wolfgang von Goethe realised, 'When Knowledge is ready to become Science, a crisis is imminent.'

In a Foreword to Ulrich Dopatka's book *Das Spiegelbild der Götter*, Däniken said it concisely and bluntly, as usual: 'Books survive the stupidity of generations.'

To say a final word about Erich von Däniken, indefatigable searcher-for-the-gods, is difficult. 'Life flows on' says it well. That is exactly true of EvD's life-work; the culmination of it is still to come.

Rainer Erler, television director and writer, knows how to evaluate extraordinary fellow-creatures. In his book *The Delegation* (a work first produced as a TV documentary, for which he won the 'Golden Camera' award), he philosophised about what is generally called 'creativity':

> Just once, sometime in every individual's life there is a faint but audible *Click*! If one's unlucky, when he's eighteen. If he's in luck, when he's sixty-five. Later, for those especially blessed.
>
> From this moment on the man is blocked from absorbing further knowledge, he's closed to all disturbing newness, no power can bring him to give up the now deep-rooted habit of thinking in straight lines. His battle against change and progress had started with that *Click*!

Erich von Däniken's *Click* is still to come. And as I know him, it will be a long time before it arrives. For he is, as his publisher von Wehren-alp recognised, 'a seeker'. He seeks the Truth.

Will he find it?

Erich von Däniken's

DOSSIER

(In his own words)

BIRTHDATE	April 14, 1935
BIRTHPLACE	Zofingen, Switzerland
ASTROLOGICAL SIGN	Aries
HEIGHT	1.68 metres (5' 6")
WEIGHT	79 kilogrammes (174 lbs)

EYES	Brown
HAIR	Brown
RESIDENCE	Tiny Cottage in Bonstetten, a suburb of Zürich
FAMILY	Wife Elisabeth, daughter Cornelia, born February 9, 1963
EDUCATIONAL DIRECTION	None. Mis-direction: Catholic. Direction of motion: Upwards
ACQUIRED PROFESSION	Waiter/Bartender/Steward/Manager/Hotelier
LANGUAGES	German, French, English, Italian and a smattering of others
AUTOMOBILE	Professional: Range Rover Family: Station Wagon
SPORT	Skiing, Idling, Looking at beautiful people
FAVOURITE FOOD(S)	Everything from my own kitchen
FAVOURITE DRINK(S)	Chateau Mouton Rothschild
HOBBIES	Surrealistic art, good Utopian literature
TEMPERAMENT	Ask my associates
WHAT INSPIRES YOU?	Intelligent, looking-to-the-future people
WHAT IRRITATES YOU?	The opposite
DAY- OR NIGHT-PERSON?	I have never understood why one should rise with the chickens
SUPERSTITION	Believer in visions
FAVOURITE AUTHOR	Miss Oesterle—ECON's book-keeper
FAVOURITE COMPOSER(S)	All who advocate 'full' sounds; no caterwauling
FAVOURITE ARTIST	The Surrealists, including Dali
MOST FASCINATING SCIENCE(S)	Palaeo-Astronautics and Exo-Biology
MOST INTERESTING HISTORICAL PERIOD	Genesis (whenever that was)
PREFERRED SEASON	Autumn
FAVOURITE COLOUR(S)	Blue and white
FAVOURITE SPOT IN SWITZERLAND	Tessin
FAVOURITE PLACE ABROAD	Tahiti
POLITICAL POSTURE	Middle-liberal. Adherent of Socialism, as long as Social achievements are

advantageous for the poor, the aged and the underprivileged. Friend of the principles of Production and Free Choice of the Individual

WHAT DON'T YOU LIKE ABOUT WESTERN SOCIETY? That 'free' Press which only uses its freedom maliciously, to destroy people or institutions

WHAT DON'T YOU LIKE ABOUT EASTERN (BLOC) SOCIETY? If I have a free choice to decide between several political systems, I'll always pick that one which guarantees me the most freedom. I want to read what I wish; I want to be allowed to say and write what I wish; and I especially want to be allowed to travel when and to where I wish (without first asking permission of some self-important lout of a Government official). As East-bloc Society grants none of these desires, my decision is obvious.

ERICH VON DÄNIKEN

This is how it was!

The real background of my prosecution

Now that a little time has passed since the event, I think I should reveal to the public the atrocious circumstances of the 'legal procedure' against me. Or should I forget the whole thing, as everyone constantly urges me to do?

Anyone who bears wounds dealt him by injustice doesn't forget. Anything else is self-defamatory sentimentality. Wounds can heal—if blockhead journalists didn't continually tear them open again with triumphant references to the 'truth' of the old stories. Or as *Playboy* and others have reduced it: an official psychiatric 'Expert Opinion' of Erich von Däniken came to the conclusion that he is a liar.

So—let's begin at the ending. On January 13, 1971, the Cantonal Government (the so-called Lower Council) took an official position on the criminal case of Erich von Däniken.

> The Lower Council considers it to be its duty to publicly express its regret that during a legal proceeding, it was attempted with presentation of inapplicable facts and personal disparagements, to put massive pressure to bear on legal agencies, and so impair trust in the Law among the public at large.
>
> With every recognition of the right to free expression of opinion, it is prescribed that this may not be misused to place the integrity of the Judiciary in doubt. The Lower Council ... thanks those of the Press who abstained from such machinations as well as all who, in spite of attempts to influence them, took care that this criminal case was carried out to its legitimate conclusion.

This professional censer-swinging was the culmination of a monstrous hypocrisy. It was meant to be assumed—and most people did so assume—that Justice had done its 'duty' and everything had proceeded in a legitimate and 'lawful' manner.

Misled by the Press, who for their part were being misused by the investigating authority, every fourth German-speaking citizen still believes today that:

1. A warrant for my arrest was issued for *misappropriation of resort taxes*, after the Davos Resort Association lodged a *criminal complaint* against me.

2. I was arrested in Vienna while trying to *make my getaway*.

3. It subsequently turned out that I had perpetrated *swindles* to the extent of about 600,000 Swiss francs, by which a whole line-up of institutions (banks) as well as private persons had been taken in.

4. The success of my books was attributable simply to the *publicity* surrounding the arrest and the trial.

5. The Swiss Federal Court (Supreme Court of Switzerland), after a thorough examination of all facts and witnesses, found the *sentence* of the Cantonal Court to be *just and proper*.

Of this widely-scattered popular opinion, which owing to circumstances I couldn't contradict, *literally nothing is true*.

1. The Davos Resort Association had *at no time* lodged a *criminal complaint* against me. (For my overdue resort taxes of about 6000 francs —senseless, as at the same time other Davos hoteliers owed a total of about 88,000 francs!)

2. I was not trying to flee, but was on my way home to Switzerland. This after previously writing two letters to the Examining Magistrate in which I informed him I would present myself for interrogation as a free man.

3. Neither bank nor other institution, let alone any private person, lodged a complaint against me. This *invention* of 'aggrieved parties' originated with then-Magistrate Hans-Peter Kirchhofer.

4. Since March 1968 my first-born *Erinnerungen an die Zukunft* (*Chariots of the Gods?*) was *No. 1 on every best-seller list* in German-speaking countries. The arrest took place on November 18 of the same year, some eight months later; success had arrived long before. The arrest and subsequent trial and sentencing brought about the exact opposite of what the Law autocratically maintained; success was not effected through this ominous court case, but the *believability of the author was basically destroyed*.

5. The Swiss Federal Court had no opportunity whatsoever to examine documents for factual content, nor to hear witnesses anew. The Federal Court is bound by the so-called 'determinations of fact' of

the lower court (the Graubünden Cantonal Court in this case). So if the lower court maintains *anything at all is proven*, the Federal court must so accept it. In practice, this means that the lower court must merely assert, where there's any doubtful item in its decision, that this or that 'fact' is proven—even when the opposite is the case—and the Federal Court is stopped cold. I'll return to this point. A Swiss thinks like this: if the Federal Court has approved a decision, they've done so after basic examination and evaluation of all circumstances, witnesses, documents, etc. The truth is otherwise.

Here is an exercise for critical readers who really want to know: Look up published decisions of the Swiss Federal Court for recent years. Analyse them. Many decisions contradict previous ones. Jurisprudence has bluntly validated the fact worldwide: Justice varies. One can no longer depend on the letter of the Law. It's according to the interpretation of the moment.

Why so?—millennia ago our forefathers knew a verbal law. Everyone interpreted this law as it suited him. Finally wise men realised: this doesn't work. So they got together and laid down the law in writing. So that everyone would know by which rules he must live, and that this law is unalterable.

This is no longer the case today. Written law is invalid for heathen, dissenters, idiots, the honest and such others who comply with it. Now the Law of Experience is the valid one.

Where the individual citizen will find the cunning to determine which Law of Experience is valid at the moment is incomprehensible. Nowadays Justice often depends on the sensibilities of some ambitious judge.

Our legal forebears thought about the future. In order to prevent individual interpretations, they phrased and paraphrased their meanings precisely. But the Davos Examining Magistrate Hans-Peter Kirchhofer, the District Attorney Willy Padrutt from Chur, and the Cantonal Court under Dr Rolf Raschein barely held to the Law as written. They made their own legal interpretations, and also knew how to put to use a complaisant Press and a blissfully-trusting Government.

To the facts.

Examining Magistrate Kirchhofer ordered a psychiatric 'Expert Opinion'. He was not concerned with the question of whether I was responsible for my actions or not. The District Attorney had no doubts on that score. So the psychiatrist Dr Erich Weber wrote to the Magistrate *before the Expert Opinion was given:*

... not been made altogether clear to me for what reasons an Expert Opinion is required. You of course know what the present situation is, and if you are really in doubt as to the accountability of the one named, I suppose I must take a deep bite into this sour apple. If you are insistent on the Expert Opinion, perhaps it would be well if we could talk it over beforehand.[1]

The purpose of this 'opinion' was kept in the background. Kirchhofer required an expert opinion which would support his own picture of me, one he had drawn in the documents of the case. But he also required an opinion which would show that the Erich von Däniken he'd arrested was wholly untrustworthy and would expose him as ridiculous. You should also know that according to the Swiss Penal Code for fraud to be established, the *intent* to enrich oneself by chicanery must be shown.[2] In addition, an intent to harm through crafty deception, or by craftily utilising another's error with intention to enrich oneself must also be demonstrated.[3]

But it was utterly impossible to impute to me a cunning 'intent to enrich myself', for during my stint as a hotelier—which was the period in question—I had continually repaid every obligation I could. But what is decisive here is that *before* I'd departed on my 1968 expedition I had given my lawyer Dr Wasch a Power of Attorney to use all income from my first book to pay off my obligations.[4] In this way any intent to 'cause harm' or to 'enrich myself' was excluded. But that didn't help; it was twisted around in a way to show that I had blindly and unscrupulously incurred debts with the deliberate intention of 'doing' my creditors. It was made to look as though it was only through the 'timely intervention of the Examining Magistrate' that the creditors ever saw their money again.

Therefore, the 'Expert Opinion' was a contrived one. The judges and the public had to be presented with a *guilty party*.

Now is a good time to emphasise the following facts: While being held for investigation I repeatedly offered to answer under narcosis ('truth drug') any and all questions concerning intent on my part to damage, and thus defraud.[5] I not only made this offer both verbally and in writing to the District Attorney and the psychiatrist, but in addition I pledged myself to take over the entire cost of this narco-analysis. Of course the offer was just as repeatedly refused. For what would have happened to the indictment, with its fabricated assertions of intention, if the truth had been established incontrovertibly in this way? (No one in the District Attorney's office granted me a hearing during the whole of my year-long investigatory imprisonment in Chur!)

Examining Magistrate Kirchhofer looked for support for the indictment. One person (Dr Weber) 'scientifically' affirmed that I had criminal tendencies. Kirchhofer was shrewd enough not to place this support for his indictment in the forefront of his strategy. (There are subtler, surer and more unassailable methods—you must captivate your audience.) District Attorney Padrutt and Assistant D. A. Emil Schmid had long been convinced by Kirchhofer of my 'dangerousness' and my 'machinations'. Finally Kirchhofer intrepidly produced a heap of documents which contained everything he wanted. District Attorney Padrutt lacked the slightest dab of civil courage, a fact which Kirchhofer in his insolence took note of. I had already been too long in confinement; the D. A. could no longer justify a retreat (a total of fourteen months held for investigation!). It didn't bear thinking what the Press might have written had I then been released.

So on May 30, 1969, a meeting took place between D. A. Padrutt, his assistant Schmid, psychiatrist Dr Weber and Examining Magistrate Kirchhofer. The latter 'oriented' the psychiatrist about the 'swindles'—any more said about this orientation would be superfluous. The result is known: a devastating 'Expert Opinion', essentially and professionally falsified, which the Law and the Lower Council were quite happy to put out as 'truth'.

I'm sorry that it's not possible to include all the details of the celebrated Expert Opinion within the framework of this contribution. For reasons of space I can merely pick parts of it to pieces, and make general observations on the 'EvD case'. I'll always be ready to dissect in similarly precise fashion any future criminal charges that may be trumped up against me.

Be that as it may, I want to pick out a few crass examples.[6]

[Page 2 of Dr Weber's Expert Opinion] This deals with the crimes of professional fraud, falsification of documents and embezzlement. The total amount in question is about 400,000 francs.

What do we really need courts for? They're not needed at all, when psychiatrist and magistrate have already decided what 'crimes' we're dealing with. The *pre*-judging is clearly evident (I wasn't sentenced by the judge until seven months after this expert's verdict). The following eight pages consisted of idle talk about my immediate family and my brother and sisters. There isn't a creditable item to be found there although, God knows, there were enough available.

On page 11 of the opinion is a portion of a letter from me to my friend Hans Neuner, torn out of context. The original letter had 6 pages.[7] Dr Weber quoted two short sentences which suited his purpose. The picture was artificially distorted.

On pages 13 to 15 my behaviour was described on the occasion of the terrible night of the Hotel Rigi-Kaltbad fire. What sort of behaviour? A complete invention of one Mr Theo Imfeld. The monstrosity of including this false description in the Opinion as alleged truth bursts into full bloom when one knows that:

1. Dr Weber had never questioned me about the night of the fire.
2. The Magistrate knew the truth, but said nothing.

[Page 15] . . . where the subject worked for a brief period in the Knorr plant, until obtaining a position with HYSPA in Bern. In this post he should have occupied the position of inn-manager. According to statements of the Examining Magistrate, certain irregularities should also have been found here which however resulted in no legal action being taken.

I 'should' have been the manager, etc. How come, 'should'? Doesn't it suit Dr Weber that I *was* the manager of the inn? About irregularities which also 'should' have been found, what's the point? Document XXIX-11 clearly states that a 'legal action is not to be taken against Erich von Däniken for crimes against property, because a police inquiry has not resulted in the slightest suspicion being cast in his direction'.[8]

Strange, that Magistrate Kirchhofer who—according to D. A. Padrutt—'only did his duty', should mislead the psychiatrist in spite of knowing the documented truth.

[Page 17] . . . and our subject accepted a position with the Blatzheim Company in Cologne. It is on the record that there he disappeared with the day's receipts of 3700 marks. The inference seems to be correct that once again we are concerned with an embezzlement.

Dr Weber prattles about 'our subject'. Interesting! And I'm supposed to have disappeared with 3700 marks, so this head-shrinker again comes to the conclusion that it's a case of embezzlement.

If one knows the records—and they were all available to Dr Weber— it's an effort to keep from breaking into hollow laughter. In fact a police inquiry yielded the information that I did not 'disappear' with 3700 marks, but on the contrary continued in my position with the Blatzheim Company.[9]

On page 19 the Expert quoted a passage from the May 26, 1969, issue of the magazine *Jasmin*—here again out of context, to falsify the sense of it. He feels a need to quote the Press. Eight months later, when the selfsame 'expert' was attacked in the Press, he wrote to attorney Hörler that press reports were 'irrelevant' to him.

[Page 20] It is safe to say that the subject is unable to manage a hotel, and that he also lacks the qualifications to fill any independent position of authority.

Lacking all these qualifications, I ask myself how I was able to hold the numerous leading positions I did, organise huge banquets, and for the three years before my arrest manage a first-class hotel. Indeed, in an objective investigation one could have questioned former employers and hotel guests. But objectivity was not desired.

On pages 23 and 24 the cat was slowly let out of the bag. Now the *author* EvD is made to look ridiculous:

Still, we'd like to let a neutral critic have his say, one who in the newspaper *Zürcher Woche* of February 29, 1969, wrote the following: As concerns the book itself, one can in view of its sales success, only remark with a smile that once again a miracle-believing mankind asks to be conned ... von Däniken's grand discovery ... must from a natural-scientific standpoint be described as a marvel of insipience and nonsense ... von Däniken's book with all its inspirations belongs in the modern class of occult and quasi-religious writings with which exceptional persons or swindlers—take your pick—try now and again to unveil for naive souls the ultimate secrets of Nature ... !

What is this tirade doing in a psychiatric opinion? Was Dr Weber commissioned to poke his nose into my books? The above quotation which the expert extracted from the *Zürcher Woche* was written by Professor Marcel Beck, a theologian with an affirmed anti-EvD bias. Beck is portrayed as a 'neutral critic'. And the objective expert Weber, among the hundreds of newspaper reviews and reports on my book *Erinnerungen an die Zukunft*, was curiously able to find only this one. Astounding.

[Page 24] While being held for investigation, the subject gave birth to a second manuscript bearing the title *Return to the Stars*. Here too we want to abstain from criticism and state only that the ideas are fantastic and could not stand up under scientific examination.

The inscrutable mind-doctor maintains that he wants to 'abstain from criticism', but abstain he does not!

[Page 25] The subject sets up unusual hypotheses . . . he reports in journalistic style, as if his hypotheses were facts . . . it would lead too far astray, were we to discuss all the themes the subject presents in his books. On page 25 of his book *Erinnerungen* . . . the subject gives a so-called basic rocket formula. He pretends to us that he obtained this formula from Professor Sänger.

I can answer that briefly: Professor Irene Sänger-Bredt sent me that formula in her letter dated August 21, 1966.

[Page 33] On 25 June 1969 he was given the opportunity to receive a visit from his wife and his daughter Cornelia. It struck us that he was unable to exhibit genuine feeling toward either wife or daughter. It was an absolutely superficial encounter.

In this stupid and clumsy manner the judges and the public had implanted in their heads my alleged emotional apathy and crudity. Just how typical is the foregoing of the whole style of this marvellous Opinion is apparent if one knows that on the evening of that visit I wrote a letter to my wife:[10]

My dearest Ebet: I thank heaven that you brought Lela to see me! You probably noticed, as I distractedly spoke with her, how I had to steel myself to keep from howling. But still, I'm very happy to have held Lela on my lap, to have looked into her eyes, to have felt her little hands, to have heard her voice. And I believe the visit did her some good too. At first the child didn't know what to make of it —now she knows again that there *is* a daddy. You and I talked at cross-purposes, as we always do on such visits. And yet it was a good visit. I hope you can come again soon. Surely sometime we'll be able to be alone again, for the imbecility of a visit under observation is so short-sighted, so petty, that afterwards one asks aghast, 'How was that possible . . . ?'

Preserve Lela from all harm for me. I want to have a happy child. I don't think much of traditional educational methods. Threats and punishment are an abomination to me; understanding, fairness and love are everything.

> your Erich.

Why do I quote this intimate letter at length? Because the letter not only went through Dr Weber's hands, and from him to the censor, but because it also bears the handwritten censor's notation of Magistrate Kirchhofer! Therefore both these gentlemen knew that the allegation about my emotional apathy was a deliberate lie. And they both kept silent about the letter's existence!

A remarkably non-psychological performance by psychologist Weber.

[Page 34] We tried to deal with the subject as generously as possible, allowing him to walk about the near vicinity accompanied by a warder. He misused this generosity by attempting to bribe the warder.

Warder Tuffli, to whom this refers, was interrogated by the police. Question: Did Mr von Däniken promise you anything, anything at all? Answer: No, absolutely nothing.[11]

[Page 39] At his places of employment, his boastfulness, desire to show off, and his criminality, led again and again first to friction, then to dismissal.

One must read this sentence several times in order to really grasp the monstrousness of it. My assembled employment references were among the documents. Once again, they were known to both Weber and Kirchhofer. And once again, they both suppressed the truth. At this point permit me to quote a few of these references:

Hotel Ascot, Zürich, December 1958: 'We were exceptionally satisfied with his work, and can describe him as an especially good waiter. He left the job at his own request.'

Hotel Europe, Davos-Platz, April 1959: '. . . Erich is a nimble waiter, well-liked by all the guests. He is a good "salesman", so that we can highly recommend him for a similar position. He left the job at the close of the season.'

Holland–America Line, December 1959: '. . . Conduct—very good; Diligence—very good; Empathy—very good.'

Hotel Europe, Davos-Platz, March 1960: 'Erich is in our house for the second time. He is an efficient *Chef de Rang*, and a good "salesman" whom we can recommend highly. He left the job at end-of-season.'

Grand Hotel, Rigi-Kaltbad, 1960: 'Erich is an efficient professional, who represents the hotel's interests. We can recommend him in every respect. He left due to end of the season.'

Grand Hotel, Rigi-Kaltbad, March 1961: 'Erich, together with his wife Elisabeth, managed our bar to our complete satisfaction. We can recommend him in every respect. His premature departure was due to the terrible fire which destroyed our house on February 8–9, 1961. We wish Erich all the best in future.'

HYSPA (Exhibition), Bern, 1961: '... Mr von Däniken proved to be a dependable support to me, his employer, and directed my entire personnel with tact and authority. He not only managed the Service and the various banquets, but relieved the burden of my own work as he also handled computations, correspondence, and in part, book-keeping. Mr von Däniken lacked no quality from either a supervisory or organisational aspect, so that subsequently he was engaged by HYSPA as managing director.'

Blatzheim Company, Cologne, February 1964: '... Mr von Däniken managed our services and banquets with cool assurance. He is efficient, has basic expertise at his disposal, and possesses a pleasing demeanour. We can recommend Mr von Däniken. Mr von Däniken left our firm voluntarily, the reason for his resignation being unknown to us.'

Restaurant Safranzunft, Basel, 1964: '... the professional abilities as well as the personal attitude of Mr von Däniken are deserving of the highest marks. Mr von Däniken is not only a versatile master of his trade, he also understands how to exert a positive influence on his co-workers and subordinates. It was a pleasure to be allowed to work with him and we can give him the highest recommendation.'

Viewing these facts, what else can one say to the Expert Opinion of Dr Weber? There are other biased passages bolstering up his views, like these:

[Page 39] In his trade he climbed from waiter to headwaiter to hotel lessee, although he possessed the qualifications from neither a moral nor a professional standpoint.

Or about my writings:

[Page 41] His incapacity to forge a genuine bond with any one discipline opened the doors for our subject to much superficial information, and led to a dilettante work of non-fiction which could at best evoke only a pitying smile from anyone trained to think scientifically.

If it went according to Dr Weber, all the scientists in the world would have summoned up only 'a pitying smile' for my books. Yet reams of facts proving the contrary are readily available.

Dr Weber crowned his affected and verbose Expert Opinion with the observation:

> [Pages 42 and 43] . . . so it is . . . not astounding that he developed into a master swindler. . . . In perpetrating the offences of which he is accused, the subject knew very well that he was transgressing against the Law. . . .

I've already said it: in Graubünden Canton courts are entirely super-fluous. Magistrates and psychiatrists arrange matters between themselves. They immediately establish what should and shouldn't be included in the case, and are sanctimoniously insulted if afterward portions of truth are brought into the open.

An abundance of further passages could be quoted, documenting the enormity of this Expert Opinion. For example, the assertion that I'm incapable of 'deep friendship'. My friends should have been asked. Or the determination that I don't possess the 'will-power to follow through'. Anyone who has written even one book knows how much faithful application is needed to finish a manuscript for the printer.

When I was allowed to read the Expert Opinion on July 17, 1969, the purpose of this coarse hypocrisy was instantly clear to me. Therefore I immediately requested higher expertise.[12] On September 30, my lawyer, Adolf Hörler, delivered a request for a supplementary Opinion to Magistrate Kirchhofer. It quoted all the essential passages in the Opinion which were, as has been shown, demonstrably false. A new request for a narco-analysis was also entered:

> I propose with the utmost urgency the execution of a superior Opinion, as Weber's Opinion proceeds from so many false premises that it must by all the laws of logic be forced to arrive at false conclusions . . .
>
> At the express wish of Mr von Däniken, I simultaneously propose conducting an interrogation under narcosis through the psychiatrist, whereby von Däniken in the presence of the defence lawyer may be asked questions decisive in these criminal proceedings.

I am aware that some time ago the Chairman of the Grand Jury of Zürich Canton decided against the introduction of such an experiment into criminal procedure because it conflicts with the inalienable rights of the individual. But on this question I refer to representative opinions in the literature, that a narco-analysis could give an indication of the innocence of one under suspicion. If this indication is ignored, it does the accused an even greater injustice, and his individual rights are even further compromised. . . .

What is feasible in any constitutional state is impossible here. The requested superior Opinion as well as the desired narco-analysis were refused on autocratic grounds through every stage of appeal. After the Examining Magistrate denied the request for another Opinion—for good reason!—we made the request to the District Attorney. Denied! To the Governing Council. Denied! We tried the Justice Court on the occasion of their General Assembly. Denied! We requested it before the Federal Court. Denied!

The Constitutional Chamber of the Swiss Federal Court said on November 4, 1970: 'As the psychiatric Opinion of Dr Weber was criticised, and it was proposed to bring in a superior expert's opinion, this could not infringe on Constitutional grievance procedure. On pages 16 to 24 of the written complaint, the objections set out in detail should have been raised in connection with the Plea of Nullity according to Article 368 of the Federal Penal Code. . . .'

But then the High Court of Appeal of the Federal Court, who had to deal with this same question of experts' opinions, wrote a week later, on November 11, 1970, verbatim:

Following the objection of the complainant, the Cantonal Court did not take into consideration favourable statements in previous documents, and was unilaterally oriented toward the latest [and *only*!] psychiatric opinion, infringing on the sphere of collection and evaluation of evidence, which, however, devolves upon the Cantonal judge, and in the Federal Court hearing on the Plea of Nullity, *can not be re-examined*.

This blatant contradiction must be obvious even to illiterates, who can nevertheless possess a sense of justice. One chamber of the Federal Court passes the decision-making buck to the other. The Feds against the Feds!

This Court makes the obscure Cantonal-court affair so easy for themselves—perfectly shown by the fact that they supported their denial of my plea by referring 53 (fifty-three!) times to the 'binding determinations' of the lower court. *Justice is not sought here, Justice is not in evidence—here Injustice is legally whitewashed.* One hand laves the other.

I feel it necessary here to say a few bitter words about Cantonal investigative methods.

There are first of all the candidly uncanny secrets of the Examining Magistrate. The smiling, priggish authoritarianism which this servant of criminal inquiry exerts against the accused and his witnesses from behind closed doors. There is a lack of any dependable check by the accused and his defence lawyer on these inquiries. And finally, the very convenient arrogance of the investigative detention procedure itself—detention wholly unnecessary where no threat to public safety exists.

To begin with, any citizen can be put in jail on the basis of suspicions and suppositions. An international warrant can be issued for his arrest. His telephone can be tapped, correspondence examined and business connections observed—on bare suppositions!—or his bank accounts sequestered.

But all of this occurs on the orders of a single person, one who is in no way impartial as to the imposition of confinement and the outcome of the trial. It is a barefaced falsehood to maintain over and over again that the Examining Magistrate's attitude toward the accused is wholly unprejudiced and objective. A magistrate has exactly the same interest in convicting the accused as does a police official. It seems necessary for me to emphasise this point especially, because in Graubünden Canton this ridiculous opinion prevails—that a defence lawyer is unnecessary during an investigation, for the rights of the accused are protected sufficiently by the Examining Magistrate. As if that very individual who wants to convict the accused had any interest in his possible innocence!

The prisoner himself is not only subjected to the torment of deprivation of freedom, but is handed over to be cut off from the outside world as a helpless and defenceless victim of the unsupervised authority of the Examining Magistrate. The single recourse remaining to him is the grievance procedure. But the Council which makes a decision on this grievance concedes a hearing neither to the accused nor to his witnesses, and sanctions the measures taken by the magistrate and/or the district attorney, both of them of course on the same team. In addition, it is then pointed out to the accused that due to his opposition or grievance petition, his time in confinement is being extended to no useful purpose. . . .

Some other details of the investigative procedure are also worth noting. The fact that the magistrate is already travelling obstinately down a one-way street is shown by the confiscation of evidence at the home of the prisoner. Everything which can be used in any way to damage him is dragged off. Anything which could cast a positive light on his person is left lying. And then the entire examination record abounds with subtly-biased questioning aimed at sealing the doom of the accused. He is represented to each witness as guilty, and the interspersed remarks and observations take care to make the witness fearful on the one hand, on the other to make him see the accused as the insidious perpetrator. If Satan is mentioned often enough—especially in financial matters—then Satan will appear.

The prejudice thus created renders the weight of evidence in the records so damning as to be ridiculous. Discrepancies which may exist between statements of witnesses and accused are used to intimidate the witness with veiled threats of prosecution for false or erroneous responses, while the accused is admonished that his 'lies' will draw a longer sentence. This kind of urging toward veracity results in false statements being made (to the prisoner's detriment) without inner conviction.

Finally, everything in the interrogations that doesn't fit into the battle-plans is omitted as insignificant or irrelevant, or in some way defused so that it's inconspicuous. And then the magistrate underlines for emphasis those portions of the hearing essential to his purpose. A like procedure is forbidden to the defence.

So the end result is a set of defective records containing errors and deliberate falsehoods, and in particular, nowhere reflecting a true picture of the personality of the accused. And the climax of this entire nauseating nonsense sailing under the banner of 'Justice' is that through the documents thus prepared, *the accused is presented to the judges as already guilty*.

This criticism of Cantonal investigative methods could apply just as well to investigative methods in other countries. Perhaps the difference lies in that a Cantonal Judge/District Attorney/Magistrate is unable to comprehend criticism. This juridical hierarchy is always and in every case infallible. Criticism verges on sacrilege and must be suppressed, especially when it stems from one criminally accused.

What do I say about the verdict now, from this point in time? The same as before: investigatory detention and trial together presented a dishonest fabrication of 'facts'. Subjective or not—even according to Swiss Law—I committed *none* of the criminal offences with which I was charged.

Article 1 of the Swiss Penal Code states: 'One can be indicted only for committing acts which the law expressly defines as punishable.' This means that the potential lawbreaker must reckon with the *written law*. Moreover, Article 18 rules that: 'Unless the Law expressly defines otherwise, one is indictable for committing a felony or misdemeanour *with malice aforethought*. A felony or misdemeanour is ... [so] ... defined, if it is executed *with knowledge and intent*.'

In the sense of the legislators, this means no more nor less than that the lawbreaker must thereupon be judged by the Court on whether he purposely committed a *crime* with knowledge and intent, or unwittingly broke an existing law with no intent to damage. (Not the *crime*, but the *deed* as such, having been committed 'with knowledge and intent'.) If we had gone along with these fundamental articles, we would never have arrived at a pre-condemnation of EvD. A malicious Expert Opinion provided the assumptions for a subsequent condemnation; for on the basis of this Opinion the judge may, and did, presume that intent to damage existed.

The Federal Court held in its decision on the Plea of Nullity on December 11, 1970, that 'Loss of Assets—where there is assumption of fraud—is already established, a claim for repayment placed in transitory jeopardy and the creditor damaged, if the debtor offers such a lower amount of security for an agreed-upon repayment that making the claim good becomes highly improbable.'

This verbal hair-splitting plainly contradicts Article 1 of the Swiss Penal Code. A most crude contradiction, for it issues from the highest judicial authority. As I mentioned at the start, judges make their own laws (*quod erat demonstrandum!*).

Just by the way, this highest court interpretation turns Switzerland into a Swindlerland, for in its terms every account not immediately paid, every pursuit, every attachment, is a 'loss of assets'. It doesn't matter that the creditor has got his money back with compound interest, or has agreed to a delay in payment. The door is opened to the arbitrary action of any individual legal officer, the fraud is an 'official offence', and suspicion alone is sufficient to start proceedings. See the case of von Däniken.

But the matter is still more amusing. The Federal Court doesn't even stand by its own decision. It sentenced me (eighteen counts!) although the debts were repaid as per agreement, in fact ahead of time, and with interest. Where the 'loss of assets' is here, or the 'transitory jeopardy', remains forever undiscoverable.

Now one reads about the most wicked miscarriages of justice in countries ruled by dictators. Switzerland is not a dictatorship. My homeland is—I recognise this with pride—the most genuine of democracies. But our political stability misleads all non-Swiss into believing that judicially also everything must operate in orderly fashion in this mini-Europe. This is a disastrous error, only realised when the ponderous machinery of Justice rolls into personal contact with an individual. That Justice rolls more obstinately, adjudicates more convincingly and apparently more objectively—but also more perfidiously.

To recapitulate: Examining Magistrate Kirchhofer and his assistants were unable to construct a straightforward case of fraud against EvD. The contrived 'incriminating material' would have trickled away like a handful of sand through a clenched fist. The guilty conscience needing whitewashing didn't belong to the accused. Therefore the accused must be kept in investigatory detention at any price, muzzled, not released on bail—true to the epigram 'We have the doer, now we'll find the deeds!' (Does anyone in Switzerland know that at the end of the investigation we offered to put up 100,000 francs bail?) Demonstrably, at the time of my arrest there were *no* deeds, no criminal acts.

Before and after sentencing, the law officials fed the Press with material deliberately and pointedly directed against me. These handouts were intended to foster the opinion that the Law had (once again) 'only done its duty', and the sole grumbler was Erich von Däniken. A tried and true measure of despotism, much simpler than honest understanding—and much worse than any fraud.

The top law officials in Graubünden conducted themselves like saints; the Magistrate was a solid mass of 'objectivity'. They dwelt in an ivory tower, hypersensitive and wearing horse-blinkers, loath to admit that the Law is just as much a public institution as transport or telephone services, and just as subject to criticism.

The Law loses all claim to respect when it acts wilfully, and labels miscarriages of justice as 'Justice'. My criminal case had as little to do with the latter as an anteater has with a computer. Injustice does not become justice because stamped as such by a higher court, nor when subsequently disseminated in a High Council communiqué as the Summit of Truth.

Before and during my time in prison none of my alleged 'injured parties' lodged a complaint against me. The legal proceedings were initiated and carried through *ex officio* by Examining Magistrate Kirchhofer. Injustice was *ex officio* allowed to arise and conquer. Switzerland to me will never be a land of Justice so long as Swiss judges and/or politicians cannot summon up the civil courage to *ex officio* redress that wrong.

The agents of the Law should impress deep in their memories what Brazilian Archbishop Dom Helder Camara said in 1968:

There is a force from which all other force derives. Force Number One. The force of injustice, which exists everywhere. When most people speak of force, they mean force Number Two, the reaction of those mishandled by injustice, the rebellion against the primary force.

Perhaps those who are angered by this account should vent their resentment upon the individuals cited here in connection with Cantonal Justice—they are force Number One.

Erich von Däniken
Bonstetten/Zürich
May 1976

NOTES

1. Letter from Dr Erich Weber, Director of the Beverin Psychiatric Clinic, to Examining Magistrate Kirchhofer; dated April 10, 1969.
2. Article 148, Swiss Penal Code.
3. Professor Dr O. Germann, *Swiss Penal Code*, 8th Edition, Schulthess Publishing Co., Zürich, 1966.
4. General Power of Attorney from Erich von Däniken to Doctor of Laws Rudolf Wäsch, Barrister and Notary, Davos, September 17, 1968.
5. Scientifically: narco-analysis. The subject lies in a twilight-sleep. His own volition—and thereby prevarication—is switched off.
6. Expert Opinion of July 12, 1969. Document No. XXXI/37.
7. Letter from Erich von Däniken to Hans Neuner, dated March 15, 1969.
8. Request to the Bern-Mittelland District Attorney, Office of the Magistrate, Examining Magistrate Hug.
9. Dossier VII.
10. Letter from Erich von Däniken to his wife, dated June 26, 1969. Document No. I/21.
11. Document No. I/235.
12. Document No. XXXI/38.
13. Verdict of the Graudünden Cantonal Court of 13 February 1970:

Erich Anton von Däniken is found guilty of repeated and continued embezzlement, repeated and professional fraud, and repeated and continued falsification of documents. He is sentenced to three and one-half years in prison, less 300 days investigatory detention, and fined 3000 francs. In addition, his civil rights are suspended for a period of two years. Court costs of 48,300 Swiss francs are to be paid by the prisoner.

ADDENDUM

Five Letters from Erich von Däniken
to his Wife Elisabeth

Written while he was imprisoned
in Regensdorf Penitentiary near Zürich 1969/70

March 6, 1969/evening

Dear Ebet:

I don't know what else to do. I've read all the books, I can't write
any more on the manuscript, and I don't keep the diary any longer for
it would only be used for some sick purpose. So I write to you.
Though I must honestly confess that I don't know *what* I should write.
I'm not allowed to report anything about this stupid affair, nor about
conditions around here because of the constant fear that—God forbid!
—someone could be insulted. So I'll just tell you how my day goes.

About half-past six is wake-up time. I make my 'toilette' and drink
my coffee. Now in a cup. Then I read till about 9, and eat something,
whatever I've put by, bread or eggs or maybe an orange. I read again
until about half-past 11 when lunch is doled out. And I read again—
sometimes I write, too—till about half-past five, supper-time. Afterward I make up the bed, sit in it and study, or now and then dictate on
tape. At 8.30 the lights go out, and I still remain sitting in bed until
around 11, then sometimes hoping to get to sleep. Often I succeed.
Oftener, I hear the clock strike one.

Afternoons at one, I'm occasionally asked if I want to walk, which
I like to do when the weather's nice. Then completely alone, I walk
around and around the courtyard like a bear in a pit. I'm happy to be
alone, for I don't know how it would go, meeting the others. Yesterday
I ran into Stauss for the first time. He was in the office where we go to
pick up things we've ordered. He kept silent, thank God, and so did I.
But today, worse luck, I met the whole gang including Stauss while
showering. I overheard a flustered Stauss telling his chums who I was,
but he still said nothing to me. I also kept silent.

Nothing happens here the entire week. I'd be happy 'without restraint' to see once more a mountain, a star or a wisp of cloud. But the Pharaoh—God keep him and bequeath him happy wives—doesn't accord me this favour. I also hope that the Pharaoh—long may he live and wisely reign—doesn't catch an Asiatic virus, as his dreams of late have led him to fear. It will really be a shock when the Pharaoh—God protect him and grant him cleverness—is forced to realise that the occupation of battling is more honourable than the malady of official-dom. As I said to you, nothing happens here. . . .

Kiss my little daughter for me. I have your and Lela's pictures always before me. Lela with the polar bear, you on the balcony. If there are later photos, you can send them with no qualms. Also without explanation. . . .

I love you and wait and trust you.

Papi

April 10, 1969

My dearest Ebetli:

It's indeed strange when one in prison has 'no time'. But this week it was actually so. On Tuesday anyway, when I was able to write. I'm going back immediately to the last chapter of the new book, which will be ready for delivery in three weeks—for everything is more or less 'on call' in my head. I'm also writing ECON and Uter-mann anew, that this book must be brought out speedily, because if Charroux hits on the same thoughts as I do—and his new book appears before mine—there'd be the devil to pay. Then I think all my protestations that I don't know Charroux's books would be in vain.

I assume you've read the report in *Spiegel*, 'Did Däniken Plagiarise?' It's a damned shame that I can't defend myself, and that my opponents can make something out of what suits them so well. This is one of the innumerable bitternesses that gnaw at me. Yet Mr Kirchhofer can only proceed with his investigation while I'm confined. . . . And over and over again the question torments me—whom have I really harmed? Society?

But let it be, because anyhow I'm only allowed to keep my silence. I would be happy—before I have a stroke or heart attack—to once again speak openly with someone without continually having to say 'no comment'. This psychological pressure that makes me ill obviously can not be measured; otherwise one would deal with it differently. In a few days I shall have a birthday. Jubilee and New Year. A conclusion and a new beginning. It's like Christmas and New Year months ago.

Always alone, always cramped, always battling with myself, always at the end of my tether, always one more time, always vanquished and always defenceless. I feel the something reaching out for me with a single cold finger outstretched. I awake bathed in sweat; my skin crawls; violet circles haunt me; my heart seems to drag along, stiff and sore; my eyes glow; joints twitch, brain throbs, and an inner trembling—indescribable, like a fivefold uneasiness—tries to tear me to pieces. But all this changes nothing. I am a 'criminal'. Birthday—bouquets—wife and child—laughter—wine—friends—tablecloth—porcelain—music—candles—thanks—feelings—understanding—handshakes—talk. Explanations, declarations, narrations—Birthday!

My dear child, do you feel for me? Then please phone my seven highly-paid barristers and ask them whether they truthfully can only 'wait'. Nothing comes from 'waiting'. Nothing—

Heartfelt thanks for chocolate and coffee and God knows what else was there. Telephone Vivel too, and pass on my thanks for the packet. What else I need—besides the newspaper clippings I asked for yesterday —is all material on Huggenberger, on Rosenhügel, on Europe, and all that's been sent to you in the past weeks and months. I need EVERYTHING. And you, dear Mampfs, please visit me again.

In inner love
your Erich

March 8, 1970

My dear Titti:

At our wedding, did you ever dream that one day I'd be writing you from prison? If I'd only accomplished all the things for which I'm in here, that would soothe me greatly. I'm here gluing conical paper bags, real paper bags. From seven in the morning till half-past eleven, and from 1.30 to 5.30. I wear a brown smock and a blue shirt without a collar. I still have my hair.

They say Regensdorf is notorious—I don't notice anything. I also don't know of anything especially worth mentioning. A prison—that's all. The officials, all the way up to the warden, make an absolutely correct impression. I see my fellow-prisoners daily in the 'circus'. That's the courtyard where we walk silently around in circles. The days crawl past, I scarcely notice. I live—with my paper bags—in another world.

Only one thing I often ask myself: Of what use, and to whom, is this entire idiocy? Who gains something from it, that I've been imprisoned for 15 months, and have another two-and-a-half years to go? I already know, after the blunder with the first confinement, that they wanted to save face. So they kept me confined because a guilty conscience wouldn't allow von Däniken to pursue his tasks; the misrepresentations in the documents would have come to light. And still now, once again a clique has to 'save face'. Therefore the excessive sentence. How many years will it take until they note in Graubünden that no face is saved using this method? Every face is made to grimace. And finally, my dearest Titti, of what use is it all? The machinations will still come out in the end.

You know, in a few years they'll be glad they listened to me. But today any talk is senseless. I'll continue: paper-bag reveries.

I love you and wait for you and Lela. Don't grind your teeth, Titti. Laugh!

always your Erich

June 21, 1970

My dear Titti:

I just now learned that the Constitutional Chamber of the Federal Court refused to grant my immediate release on the grounds that I would 'gain advantage' from it. It's incomprehensible to me what kind of 'advantage' would accrue, but I know with certainty that the District Attorney's Office doesn't want to let *their* advantage—namely my encapsulation—out of their hands at any price. That would be terrible, I'd be able to defend myself! Shocking, I'd be able to give interviews! Unthinkable, a free Däniken, after he's been so-o-o beautifully convicted and sentenced.

It's also clear that we can hope for no honesty from the Federal Court. For why should the Court want to meet me halfway on even a single point, why examine a single item neutrally and objectively, when the pre-judging—leaving me imprisoned—is already signed and sealed?

Somewhere during the past weeks I picked up a little story I'd like to pass on to you: A self-willed teacher in a Russian school said to the children, two times two is nine. The little ones ran outside and trumpeted in schoolyard and at home, two times two is nine! At a hastily-called teachers' conference the school director advanced the opinion that the truth should not be too suddenly revealed to the minor children, but that they might be cautiously and gradually prepared for it. So a new teacher came to class and with a straight face announced to the laughing urchins: two times two is seven. Some of the children piously and stupidly scribbled this figure in their notebooks. Others defiantly scrawled the old one on toilet-walls and slates: two times two is nine! There were even children who shouted, two times two is one! Then, when after a few weeks the teacher came a little nearer the truth and asserted that two times two is five, the children winked slyly at each other, and laughed about school, teacher, rector and conference. They wrote the wildest solutions all over the streets, and disconcerted their parents with: two times two is eight! Or two times two is zero!

In truth, however, not one of the little ones had ever doubted, that twice two is four, for the truth could be counted on their fingers.

You may sleep in peace, dear Switzerland, your make-believe world is still in order.

Can YOU, my dear wife, ease my heart and inform me *how* I'm supposed to have 'betrayed' Dr Stehlin? Or Mo? Or the bank fellows? That was already 200,000 francs, the alleged swindle. If not, then let us wait. This secret will probably be angrily publicised from Chur one day. Only if I'm defenceless, of course.

Ciao, Schatzi. I'd love to be with you
now. Many kisses & heartfelt greetings.
your Erich

July 5, 1970

My dear Titti:

Only the best for your birthday! It shall be better, when I'm once again allowed to be a man. I want to try to realise a reasonable portion of your dreams. As a birthday present from these walls, I beg you: TAKE DRIVING LESSONS! There are women for whom driving lessons are no gift. It all depends on the results.

Today the film *Chariots of the Gods* will be shown here. A strange feeling, not to have seen your own film-footage yet. I just don't know how closely the camera crew followed my suggestions. It was filmed without me, because I wasn't available. It all depends so much on details. Possibly my absence during filming will result in some child's game played around Däniken. Sabotage made easy!

Nothing new with me. Now as before I'm in the garden, and gradually getting a clue about tomatoes, onions, leeks, beans and other weeds. Letters from readers never cease. Are you answering all you get? I've also heard that another anti-me book is being written. Peculiar, that these 'fair' authors don't have a single question to ask me. They apparently know me better than I know myself. And then that envious babble about plagiarism! Strange in this connection too, that it didn't occur to a single one of these heroes to write me a note and pose me a few plain questions. I wouldn't have hesitated to answer.

It will all be briskly and happily besmirched, belied, bespangled and begarbled. Däniken is in quod, he can't defend himself. Hallelujah!

with all my heart, always your
Erich

Index of Names